Magic Box Paradigm

A framework for startup acquisitions

Ezra Roizen

Edited by Bambi Francisco Roizen

ANTOINE - I HOPE THIS HELPS
YOU IN YOUR NEW ROLE!

EZRA

advsr ideas

Advsr, LLC
875-A Island Drive #255
Alameda, CA 94502

ISBN: 0692778047
ISBN 13: 9780692778043

Thanks to

Bob Krupp; without you, I would never have gotten into this business

and

Mike Ackrell; without you, in it I wouldn't have lasted very long.

Join the Conversation

This book is intended to be the start of a broader discussion.

If you have additional questions you'd like to ask or ideas you'd like to share please visit our website and post a comment:

www.advsr.com/mbp

Our team at Advsr is going to expand on the Magic Box Paradigm in blogs, essays and maybe even future books. We'd enjoy your feedback and input.

We look forward to hearing from you!

Acknowledgments

The following people contributed a great deal to the enhancement and refinement of this book:

Ron Roizen, independent scholar, Roizen.com
Gaurav Mathur, partner, Silicon Legal Strategy
Andre Gharakhanian, partner, Silicon Legal Strategy
Heidi Roizen, operating partner, DFJ
Sebastian Rupley, senior writer, eBay
Daniel Friedland, managing partner, Goldcrest Capital
Sam Angus, partner, Fenwick & West
Patrick Chung, cofounder, Xfund
Laura Medina, partner, Cooley
Eric Jensen, partner, Cooley
Michael Ackrell, managing partner, Ackrell Capital
Demian Entrekin, advisor, Advsr
Erin Flynn, advisor, Advsr
Alex Roizen, advisor, Advsr

Thanks to all of you!

I'll give thrice so much land to any

well-deserving friend;

But in the way of bargain, mark you me,

I'll cavil on the ninth part of a hair.

—Hotspur, *Henry IV, Part 1* (William Shakespeare)

Contents

Introduction

What if I told you that the last thing you want from a potential acquirer is a term sheet? Or that the casualty of a bidding war is most likely going to be you? Or the presentation you use when you meet with investors is almost the opposite of the one you should use with strategic partners? Or that acquirers' efforts to reduce their risk when making an acquisition can often increase the likelihood of their failure?

Startup acquisitions are counterintuitive. Many of the moves your intuition would lead you to make are wrong. These bad moves can hurt, or kill, a deal.

The good news is—once you've absorbed this book—you won't be one of the mistake makers. This book is going to give you a framework for attracting acquisition interest, and if you choose to pursue being acquired, it's going to show you how to optimize and close the deal.

To understand a bit more about the origin and context of this book, read the last section: Backstory. To get right into it, simply turn the page.

Prologue

We'll begin with an irrefutable truth: Startup acquisitions fall apart all the time. There are, however, reliable ways to lessen the likelihood that your deal will.

The Magic Box Paradigm (MBP), the approach articulated in this book, will enhance your ability to optimize and complete a good deal. The MBP will also direct you away from a bad deal and mitigate the damage of a failed one.

Upside with no downside!

To have a good beginning you have to understand a bad end

Let's start our journey with the story of a deal that didn't close.

Startup Alpha receives some relatively serious-sounding inbound acquisition interest. This interest is coming from a buyer we'll call BigCo. Alpha's founder calls a board meeting to discuss the opportunity. Several board members believe that now is a good time to sell but also feel a better deal could be found.

Alpha engages the services of an investment banker to scout out a few other potential buyers. The investment banker is given responsibility for all potential buyers, including BigCo, who's already expressed some real interest.

The banker moves fast, drives hard and attracts a couple of additional buyers. However, these new potential buyers are feeling rushed and ill equipped to move quickly. After all, they're contemplating acquiring a brand-new technology based on an acquisition thesis they haven't fully developed.

The banker communicates to BigCo that there are several other interested parties, and they will need to improve their offer if they are going to win the deal.

In light of this circumstance, BigCo develops a term sheet. The term sheet has an increased price from the original indication and outlines the rough dimensions of the deal. The term sheet also contains a "no-shop" provision. This provision provides BigCo with a sixty-day exclusive period during which Alpha promises to discontinue all conversations with other potential buyers.

The justification BigCo uses for needing this sixty-day exclusive period is that they now know other potential buyers are in the wings. And BigCo is unwilling to commit the necessary time and resources to the transaction if there's a chance they will lose the deal to another suitor. They also explain that because everything has happened so quickly, they need the full sixty days to complete their due diligence.

Alpha's board of directors, founder and management team are nervous because other buyers haven't quickly jumped into the fray, and decide to move forward with BigCo. They sign the term sheet with BigCo.

In order to comply with the exclusivity provision of the term sheet, Alpha ceases conversations with other potential bidders. A flurry of meetings with an ever-increasing number of Startup Alpha's and BigCo's team members ensue. Alpha's investors are excited about the prospect of an exit with a pretty handsome return. The team is already online checking out new cars. Everyone is pumped.

But then, meetings with BigCo slow down. Long days separate increasingly infrequent interactions. No one is looking in Alpha's data room. At Alpha's board meeting, the founder is asked if there is a target closing date and if a draft of the definitive agreement has been received from BigCo's attorneys. There isn't, and one hasn't.

It's been five weeks since the term sheet was signed, and yet a deal doesn't seem any closer to closing than when the process started. The other interested bidders are long forgotten. Alpha's team members are asking questions. The investors are getting antsy.

Then Alpha's founder gets an e-mail from BigCo:

> *Do you have time for a quick call tomorrow?*

This is what's said by BigCo on the call (I know, because it's said on every one of these calls):

> *Hey, thanks for taking the time to hop on the phone. I really want to thank you and your team for the effort they've put into this discussion. When we initially engaged in all of this a few months ago, there was a great deal of excitement about this direction. However, we've had some changes in priorities on our end, and it looks like this initiative is losing out to some other projects our executive team has elevated. I'm really sorry, but we won't be moving forward with this acquisition at this time, although we'd love to stay in the loop as you progress. Let's reconnect in a couple of quarters. Thanks again! You guys are great!*

The person on the BigCo end of the call hangs up and feels relieved. It was all getting to be too much to handle. And, clearly, the deal had lost internal support. She's onto her next task and might even be able to get in a round of golf with all the time that's been freed up by not having to support the acquisition process.

Alpha is left out in the cold. The problems for Alpha's founder are greater than just the failed deal. First, he has to break the bad news to his team, his board and his investors. Everyone was very excited about doing a deal, and its failure will be a momentum killer. On top of that, he now has no alternative buyers lined up. Worst of all, the first thing any previously interested, potential buyer is now going to ask is, "Why didn't so-and-so end up completing the deal? Did they find something wrong?"

Alpha's founder isn't just back at square one, he's back at square negative ten. Cold porridge is for dinner.

How could this have happened?

Pretty easily, actually. Here's the view from BigCo's side.

Alpha was on BigCo's radar. The latter was thinking that Alpha could fill a gap in BigCo's product portfolio. It seemed easier to acquire Alpha than build a team to develop essentially what Alpha already had. BigCo's head of product development, a charismatic and energetic executive, articulated the case beautifully to the internal team.

There was certainly some real momentum at the outset. The idea of buying a cool startup is exciting. BigCo's divisional general manager was intrigued, and the corporate development team from headquarters was engaged to help the product manager figure out what was possible.

Then, out of the blue, BigCo's corporate development lead gets a call from Alpha's investment banker. The banker is clearly shopping Alpha to all comers. BigCo feels the pressure tick up. The only thing worse than losing a deal is to lose it to a competitor.

BigCo's corporate development lead is feeling rushed. He pulls up the term sheet from the last deal, which was for buying a factory. He tries to customize it for use in this new startup situation. He adds an extended no-shop provision, since at this point his team knows almost nothing about the startup and they need time to get up to speed.

There's a thrill-of-the-deal moment.

At the same time, there's some consternation on BigCo's part about how the process is unfolding. It's kind of annoying to deal with Alpha's investment banker. It's a bit disappointing that Alpha is seeking other suitors. It's also now apparent that BigCo is going to have to pay more for Alpha than they originally thought. But, since BigCo's product development head loves the idea and it looks like some of BigCo's competitors may like Alpha as well, maybe the deal's still worth it? Who knows?

The term sheet isn't binding on BigCo anyway, so BigCo's corporate development lead recommends that they "lock them up now and then figure out if this is a deal we want to do later."

A clunky, vague, term sheet—one that does little to clarify the terms of a potential deal—is executed. It includes the sixty-day, no-shop provision. BigCo has bought some precious time.

Alpha's and BigCo's product teams come together. It turns out there are a few key architectural differences between their platforms. Also, the startup's head of engineering is a "bit of a kook."

BigCo's corporate development lead takes a quick look at the financial folders in Alpha's data room. Most of Alpha's revenue comes from some old product that is of no interest to BigCo; the remainder of Alpha's revenue is mostly coming from a customer that's also of no interest. Things aren't quite perfect.

Meantime, BigCo's executive team is heading off next week for a weeklong planning off-site. The head of product really needs to wait for the results of that meeting before she can make progress on the deal. This delay adds weeks to the time since the term sheet was signed.

Once the executive team returns, it's clear the priorities they set at the off-site meeting are not exactly in line with the thesis for this acquisition.

But the head of product pushes on. She prepares the case for the executive team. She emphasizes the pro-purchase thesis but also, and in fairness, notes some of the issues they've discovered too.

BigCo's corporate development lead did his job: He locked up Alpha in a binding exclusive period. However, he isn't particularly excited about buying a startup that isn't profitable. Plus, he still has a bit of a bad aftertaste from the term sheet negotiation. He points out the negative issues in the business model and current revenue dynamics. Even though they are pretty much irrelevant to the head of product's case for acquiring Alpha, negatives seem to be piling up against the prospective deal. The tide is shifting.

After a long discussion with the team, BigCo's general manager decides the deal is more expensive than they anticipated. Too many nettlesome issues have come up. And, frankly, the deal is no longer fully in line with the overall priorities that emerged from the recent executive off-site.

The decision is made to discontinue pursuit of the acquisition.

This scenario plays out over and over again, day in and day out, in startup land. Yet, it can be entirely avoided.

Chapter 1

The Popsicle and the magic box

It's not about selling your company; it's about creating opportunities for your startup to be acquired

I chose the words "creating opportunities for your startup to be acquired" very carefully. I don't start with the assumption that you will necessarily sell your company. Nor do I recommend an approach that zeros in on and drives toward, a single, ultimate outcome. Quite the contrary. I want you to position yourself to be acquired, should you choose to be.

In parallel with developing inbound acquisition interest, I also want you to spark interest in commercial partnerships and even investment, from the same potential strategic partners.

To save on ink, we're going to shorten the term potential strategic partners to "PSP." And, by way of clarifying the term, for our purposes here, PSPs are the large operating companies in relevant industries, who represent access to considerable growth resources for your startup—be it through commercial relationships, investment or outright acquisition.

Should it come to pass that you decide that the highest and best use of your startup is most likely achieved in full combination with a PSP, it will be a very good thing that you have cultivated an environment where there are a number of them who would enthusiastically entertain a discussion of potentially acquiring it.

Startups are bought, not sold

Everyone knows the adage: "Companies are bought, not sold." Though it's not entirely true, as certain companies can be pretty successfully sold, there is no truer principle when it comes to startups: They do indeed have to be bought, and they are very hard to sell.

That startups have to be bought should not be taken to mean that you shouldn't be proactive or that you can't influence events and create momentum. This book is all about proactiveness, influence and acceleration.

The important difference between selling and being bought can be made clear by comparing Popsicles with magic boxes.

Popsicles are sold

It's a hot day on the beach. You hear the bell of the Popsicle seller. You know the exact utility of the Popsicle. It's going to cool you down and by holding one you're going to look like a fun person. Popsicles also have a known and narrow range of possible prices. The supply and demand dynamics are clear for all to see. If the Popsicle vendor ventured deep onto the beach, you might be willing to pay a small premium to keep your feet from getting burned hopping across the sand. However, if the Popsicle vendor happens to be between three other Popsicle vendors, the price premium quickly melts away.

The Popsicle has a defined nature, a similar value to each buyer (it's equally cool and refreshing to everyone!), a clear market, and the purchase of it is completed instantaneously.

These same basic dynamics apply to many asset classes, like real estate, restaurants and parking lots. They have a calculable value and a market that is pretty clear. Usually a seller of these kinds of assets can present the same offering to all prospective buyers, as the nature of the opportunity and its utility are common to everyone. A prospective buyer can look closely at metrics, like historical performance and market comparables to define what they feel to be a fair market price, and make an offer.

If the seller receives multiple offers, there's an opportunity to run an auction process to find the buyer willing to pay the most. Once the highest bid is made, the parameters of the transaction are easily clarified and a sale promptly closed.

Further, for many asset classes, there are ways for the seller to incrementally bind the buyer to the deal. Deposits, or as they are aptly named in this business, "earnest payments," are a simple example of a seller tool for binding a buyer. Deposits transfer power from the buyer to the seller and serve to increase the buyer's commitment to completing the transaction.

You can sell things when you can present the same opportunity to the market, provide guidance on pricing, run an auction, incrementally get the chosen buyer increasingly committed to the transaction, and quickly close the deal.

Startups are an altogether different object

Let's swap out the Popsicle and in its place put a magic box.

In the hands of some owners, every time the magic box is opened, inside can be found one hundred gold coins. In the hands of other owners, when they open the box, they find ten silver coins. In the hands of the least compelling owners, every opening of the box only yields a lump of coal.

The value of the box varies significantly from buyer to buyer and as such each will view its importance differently.

Let's add two more twists. Let's say the magic box can only be physically opened by the original owner, even after it's sold. And, let's say that in order to be opened, the original owner and the new buyer have to carry the magic box to the top of a mountain.

To summarize the view from across the table: I'm the potential buyer of a box that might magically yield some number of gold coins or might not. This magic box can only be opened by the person selling me the box, and after I buy it, together we are going to journey up a mountain before I know what it's worth.

In other words, I have to put a great deal of faith into both this person and this box.

Startups are more like magic boxes than Popsicles

When an acquirer is buying a startup, they are usually buying a technology that is still in process, and they probably need to retain the team to continue its development. Before they can see value from the technology, it's likely going to have to be integrated into their existing products and distribution channels.

The buyer has to pay for the magic box (your startup), retain the seller to open it (your team to continue to develop the technology), and fund the postpurchase expedition to get the box to the top of the mountain (integrate it into their offerings and distribution channels)!

This is why startups are like magic boxes. Unfortunately, they're often approached as if they were Popsicles.

Making matters worse, unlike in the sale of many other assets—where sellers incrementally gain commitment and leverage—in startup acquisitions, the balance of power between buyer and seller is massively shifted toward the buyer.

An example of how power is shifted from seller to buyer in startup acquisitions is the exclusive period. Rather than having the seller-friendly “earnest payments” we described above, in startup acquisitions, the first course of action for many buyers is to lock up the seller by locking out other suitors. As noted in the prologue, exclusive periods are binding to the seller but do nothing to ensure the earnestness of the buyer. The seller is prohibited from speaking to alternate buyers before receiving any tangible commitment from the one across the table. The buyer, on the other hand, is free to explore other options, change the deal, or do nothing at all.

The sum of all of this is that startup acquisitions are much more challenging than the sale of Popsicles. For starters, because the value of the startup can vary significantly from buyer to buyer, it’s nearly impossible to communicate a single price to the market. Then, since price dynamics (among other key acquisition priorities, like varying views on the importance of retaining various team members) are different between buyers, it’s exceedingly difficult to run auctions. Added to this is the reality that there are few tools for incrementally binding buyers to a deal. And then, if all of this weren’t enough, the deals themselves are extremely complicated and difficult to close. This deal-complexity means that the risk a startup takes when committing to any single buyer for an extended closing period is significant. Buyers change their mind and scuttle acquisitions all the time.

Other than that Mrs. Lincoln, how was the play?

There is a different way things can play out. But in order to change the game, your prospective buyer must believe in your magic box, must trust you and your team, and must be willing to fund your joint expedition to the top of the mountain. In turn, you must believe that the buyer will, in fact, find gold.

If you can establish this shared belief and mutual trust, then there are ways to proactively create opportunities for your startup to be acquired, and many techniques you can employ to increase the likelihood of close.

In fact, several of the forces working against you when you take a Popsicle-selling approach can be turned in your favor when you embrace the notion that you are instead dealing with a magic box. But for this to happen, the approach you take has to be holistic. You have to use the Magic Box Paradigm.

Chapter 2

It's how you enter the room

Most startups consider their growth strategies in a largely sequential way: I'm out raising money. I'm building commercial partnerships. I'm for sale.

What if they are all in play all the time? Rather than just articulating one approach, why not introduce yourself to PSPs the following way:

> *We're an innovative company looking for the resources we need for growth. Those resources may come in the form of investment capital; they may come through commercial partnerships (for example, access to broader distribution and/or more effective methods of monetization), or it may be that the best way for us to gain the resources we need to fulfill this opportunity is in full combination with a larger player through an acquisition. We're opportunistic.*

Even inside of these three tracks, there are any number of hybrid models. You could consider taking investment, and in parallel establish a significant commercial partnership; or maybe stay operationally independent but sell a majority stake; or maybe spin off part of your company and raise capital for that new entity—the list goes on.

Don't single-thread your thinking. Be opportunistic and attune to creative places to find resources. Enter the room with an inquisitive mind and have open-ended conversations once you're in there.

You are not more for sale than any other startup, but every startup is for sale

Once you take venture capital or give an employee a stock option, you are trading current economic value for future return. Venture capital firms plan to eventually sell some or all of their position. The reason your employees are taking below-market salaries is because they someday plan to make money on their stock options.

A small percentage of startups will be so successful that their investors, founders and employees will be able to liquidate some or all their equity positions in the late-stage private capital secondary markets, or in the public markets. These are the companies that are able to get their magic box to the top of the mountain on their own. This book is less for them, and more for the startups who are potentially going to need to team up to unlock the full power of their magic box.

For the vast majority of startups, the path to equity return is going to be through acquisition. I say “equity return” because there are lots of businesses that operate simply to make increasing profits, and the returns to owners and employees are realized through dividends and profit sharing. What a thought! However, in the startup world, we’re optimizing in many different ways for return on equity: From venture capital to stock options (and many elements in between), the business of startups is built around an increasing value of equity, and the eventual sale of that equity.

Value is created when there is the potential for growth

Being small with big potential is much better than being big with small potential.

Recently a large grocery chain, with around 150,000 employees, was acquired for approximately $8 billion. Around the same time, a startup with around fifty employees was acquired for approximately $16 billion.

That's twice as much! Said differently, a price-per-employee of roughly $50 thousand for the grocery chain, and of $300 million per employee for the startup—a six thousand times difference.

In broad strokes, I think it would be reasonable to assume that the startup was seen as being poised for significant growth, and in the grocery chain's case, value was more likely going to be created by optimizing offerings and making incremental improvements to operations.

To be clear, this is not to say that the number of employees is a key factor in valuation. In this case, I'm just using the number of employees to give a sense of the size of each enterprise and the magnitude of the difference in value ascribed to companies that are perceived to have a great deal of growth in front of them.

The potential for growth drives value. But there are many ways for a startup to grow. It may be the case that your startup can grow faster and thereby create value sooner as part of a larger corporation.

Snowballs and avalanches

Startups usually start small. They are typically founded by close-knit teams working in sync to create a new innovation. However, once created, the best way to bring the new offering to market may be quite different from the style in which it was invented.

It may not be a small team or a can-do, do-it-yourself approach that is best. The new offering may just make more sense when plugged into existing distribution channels or may actually be best leveraged as a component of a larger platform. There may be many compelling reasons why a new offering makes more sense being commercialized in concert with a PSP.

This is because the challenges of being small and independent are numerous. For example, there are many new innovations that consumers want to use, but for which they don't want to pay! Or if you can charge, the act of inserting a toll booth alters the flow of the user experience so profoundly it will stunt the growth of the offering and give way to a better-funded competitor, able to forestall its monetization just a bit longer. In other cases, the cost of sale is so large, and the sales cycle so slow, that it will require much greater resources than the startup has available to build an effective sales organization.

Sometimes products can be adjusted to account for these challenges, but those adaptations (to enable distribution or monetization) have commensurate implications and costs.

Everything comes at a price. Strategy is about finding the optimal balance of the various competing forces.

Product, distribution and monetization

Let's posit that there are three primary forces at work in a startup's strategy, and that the interplay of these three forces typically represents the various trade-offs the startup must make as it rolls out new innovations. These forces are:

- Product
- Distribution
- Monetization

Typically startups are very strong in product (what they are building), have some initial understanding of distribution (how they will get it to customers) and are early in their thinking around monetization (how they plan to make money).

Raise capital, establish commercial partnerships, be acquired

Let's now posit a second dimension how a startup accesses the resources it needs for growth:

- Raise capital
- Establish commercial partnerships
- Be acquired

Raising capital typically consumes most of the thinking and energy a startup puts into resource accumulation. But it's not the only path.

Ultimately, most of the growth capital a typical startup raises goes into distribution (getting their product into customer hands, one way or another). For many startups, there are established companies that already have distribution channels into their likely customers. If the startup were able to set up commercial partnerships with these companies in order to access those distribution channels, they would need to raise less capital, and their mix of required resources changes.

However, in commercial partnerships, it's difficult to align brands, integrate products and share profits. Because of this, outside of the efforts of a plucky business development lead grabbing low-hanging fruit, deep commercial partnering often isn't viewed by startups as a reliable path for consistent growth. For the startups able to take this path to market, however, they would likely see a reduction in the amount of capital required to develop distribution channels. For now, just hold that thought.

In theory, acquisitions are the ultimate partnership: All the benefits, with none of the friction. The startup and acquirer can fully integrate their offerings, optimize economics and present a united product to the market. They are ways for the startup to accumulate significant resources and probably get to market faster.

For the purposes of this book, let's think about acquisitions from the mind-set of the accumulation of the resources your startup needs for growth—an alternative alongside raising capital or commercial partnerships. For startups, we'll consider an acquisition to be an "entrance" into the resources you need rather than an "exit" from the resources you've already accumulated.

If we map the two dimensions we discussed above, we get the following startup resource accumulation typology:

Startup resource accumulation typology

	Raise capital (Stay independent)	**Establish commercial partnerships**	**Be acquired (Fully combine)**
Product	Complete product suite	Logical integrations with commercial partners	Technology that can extend offerings
Distribution	Ability to create independent distribution channels	Ability to unlock opportunities and create dependencies	Significant leverage from existing channels
Monetization	Intrinsic and effective monetization	Easily attainable companion monetization	Dramatically improved in combination

If you have a complete product suite, can create your own independent distribution channels, and have intrinsic and effective monetization (you can make money on your own), then it's very likely that your best growth strategy is raising capital and going it alone. Crank the flywheel of positive unit economics. Strap your magic box on your back. Get it to the top of the mountain!

If you have logical integrations with PSPs that can be clearly defined, easily implemented, and yield compelling returns for both you and the commercial partner, then there's an opportunity for you to grow through commercial partnerships. Further, there's a good chance that the best of these commercial partners will develop a deep appreciation of your strategy and offerings. In some cases, dependencies on your platform will form, which should yield benefits both commercially and strategically.

If you come to realize that you've created a compelling innovation, but the cost to develop the next phase of your distribution channels or your ability to independently monetize your offering are significantly enhanced in combination with a larger player, then you should be anticipating that it's highly likely your optimal, long-range growth strategy is to be acquired.

For some startups, the optimal strategy isn't always clear. There may be a variety of perspectives or strategic biases that complicate the discussion. Engaging in a balancing of forces conversation both internally among your stakeholders and externally with relevant investors and PSPs will sharpen your thinking and shed light on any number of otherwise unconsidered dimensions to your strategy.

Chapter 3

The Magic Box Paradigm

The MBP is the holistic framework for creating, and executing upon, acquisition opportunities for your startup. The MBP is based on the first principles that startup acquisitions are:

- Buyer driven rather than seller driven
- A way for startups to access the resources they need for growth and should be approached as "entrances" rather than "exits"
- Dependent upon valuations specific to each buyer-seller pairing
- Intricate and as such need to be designed with precision and handled with care

Remember this

If we apply the MBP, we see the emergence of three practical realities.

First, startup acquisitions are driven by a big idea, an idea so big the buyer has to own your startup to see it fulfilled. But, the trick is, it has to be their big idea.

Second, the complexity of startup acquisitions has fundamental and profound implications on the way they must be approached. This complexity impacts every part of the process—from start to finish.

Third, these things take time, and most startups wait far too long before they start developing meaningful relationships with PSPs.

Big companies would rather not buy startups

For big companies, acquisitions are hard. They are expensive, highly visible and risky. If there is a way to avoid making an acquisition (commercial partnership, licensing agreement, etc.), most big companies will opt to take the path of least resistance. For the most part, they only buy startups when they believe they have no other way to get where they believe they need to go.

The big idea

What drives startup acquisitions is a big idea. An idea so big and so powerful that the only way the PSP feels the idea can be realized is with the acquisition of your startup.

But it has to be their idea. The idea has to be built from their organizational DNA, articulated in their language and aligned with their corporate mission and values.

Inside and out, the idea has to be theirs.

Creating the space for the big idea

God spoke the universe into existence. He didn't present it into existence, financial model it into existence or SWOT it into existence. He spoke it.

The first big idea was spoken. And so have been all others since. Words are important. People think in narrative. But in your case, since you're most likely not a deity, the process has to be a bit more subtle. You can't walk in with a complete picture as you'll leave no room for the buyer to come up with the idea on their own. The delicate art of catalyzing big ideas is in putting enough of the parts on the table so that the idea creator has all the material they need to form the whole.

A common mistake startups make is to use one of their two existing dominant narratives when they have conversations with PSPs. Startups have usually created one narrative for potential investors and another narrative for potential customers. Very often, neither of these narratives is just right for PSPs. Their problem is their completeness.

The challenge with venture capital–oriented narratives

Venture capitalists (VCs) can offer wisdom, access and advice, but they really only have one economic tool at their disposal: cash. VCs can't round out your product offerings, nor provide you with distribution channels, nor enhance your ability to monetize your customers.

As such, when you go and talk to a VC, you have to have it all figured out. The entire story has to seamlessly fit together. All you need is their cash, and with it you can roll out a series of complete products, cost effectively reach consumers and extract impressive gross profits. Your customer lifetime value (CLV) is clearly going to dwarf your cost to acquire a customer (CAC). When you go to VCs, you present yourself in as complete a form as possible.

PSPs already have customers. They have existing product offerings and established distribution channels. They have a certain way they like to structure their revenue models. Walking in with it all figured out means you're almost assuredly going to have a mismatch with something they approach differently. To PSPs, you are just a piece of a puzzle to be combined with other pieces to create the complete picture.

They, for the most part, have a much better view of where you best fit into their master plan. You're a blue puzzle piece, which you think looks perfectly suited to become part of the sky. They, however, may have already pegged you to be part of the ocean. Better to describe your blueness than prescribe where you fit, and get it wrong.

For most startup acquisitions, what you do is at most an 80 percent match to what the PSP is looking to accomplish, and often more like 20 percent. Acquiring you will advance them down the road, not get them to the destination. You are a means to their ends.

The trick is saying enough to articulate a vision of the future and your current strategy but not to say so much that it stunts their participation in the conversation. Creating the big idea is an effort in cocreation where you are the copilot. Let them fit what you are into what they think they want.

The challenge with product-oriented narratives

At the other end of the spectrum, startups focus the conversation with the PSP on the features and benefits of their current product. This approach does a fine job of articulating capabilities and explaining how well the product solves specific problems but doesn't paint a picture of a larger mission and direction. In conversations with PSPs, your product shouldn't be the entire story but instead be presented as the initial manifestation of a larger journey, a journey which maps to a massive shift in the market.

You have to set the context. Discussing your product simply as it stands today is like trying to explain an entire television series by only discussing the first episode. The meta narrative and arc of the story are completely lost.

Similar to the challenge with VC narratives we discussed above, product-centered narratives tend toward completeness. The product has all the answers, and when something comes up for which the product doesn't currently have an answer, the question is either deemed irrelevant as a feature for only the backward and dimwitted, or the capability is already on the product roadmap and scheduled for the next release. Product-focused presentations often leave little room for collaborative thinking.

Resist the urge to have all the answers

You're an entrepreneur. You're a brilliant, confident, risk-seeking, new-economy warrior. You're not Type A. You're Type A+. You have all the answers for your investors, customers and employees. You've got this thing figured out. You're way ahead of the curve.

Now, I'm going to throw you for a loop. You have to unfigure it all out. You are going to have to uncondition yourself when you approach PSPs. Remember! For this to work, it has to be their idea, not your idea. You're going to have to turn on your "what part of this do they like?" radar. They are going to drop hints and signals. If you're too busy telling them all the answers, you'll miss them.

Having all the answers kills idea formation. Seeming set on a specific path can make you seem inflexible to changing direction (and it's almost a certainty that your and their directions are not exactly the same). Worst of all, appearing to have it all figured out can make you seem arrogant.

If the PSP's idea formation is stunted, and they start to think you're heading in a different direction, and you come across as a bit too arrogant to fit in their organization, then that's three strikes and you're out.

What you want to be is confident, open-minded, collaborative, easy to work with, fun, inquisitive and curious. Don't have all the answers. Listen, pick up the clues, and most of all, be humble.

The complexity of these transactions has profound implications

It's hard to understate the complexity of startup acquisitions.

This complexity has implications on everything: from optimizing price, to risk sharing, to definitive agreements, and in many deals, the hangover of the complexity lives on for years after the deal is closed.

I've been fortunate to have been an advisor, friend, investor or observer to more transactions between startups and strategic partners than I can remember. I've seen lots of deals come together, and more importantly, I've seen even more deals fall apart.

If I had to distill all the failed deals down to one root cause, it would be complexity. The number of people needing alignment on both sides of the table (some with whacky demands!), nuances of the thesis for the acquisition, economics, legal structure, team retention, due diligence, risk allocation and so on, all consume time and lead to the gradual decay of the original energy and momentum for getting the deal done in the first place.

Once the high-level terms of a deal have been set, I peg the chances of the deal actually closing at about fifty-fifty. Think how incredible that is: Two companies have come together to agree on a product strategy, agree that it makes sense to join forces (forever!), and have even sorted out high-level economic terms, and yet there's still only a fifty-fifty shot that the deal will end up being completed. Very often, momentum is lost, or something comes up and the deal is abandoned.

Once lawyers are involved and definitive agreements are underway, I put the probability it closes at around eighty-twenty. But there's still a one-in-five chance that something will blow up the deal.

My guidance goes up to 100 percent once the deal is completed, and the money is in the bank.

The one constant in startup acquisitions is that they are completely inconsistent. They fall apart all the time for all kinds of reasons.

Anticipating complexity has to inform the other elements of your acquisition strategy. These transactions have to be approached holistically, with the process of closing them considered from the start. Like a logic problem, work them from both ends. From the acquisition thesis forward, and the completed transaction backward.

More often than not, you will be better off resisting the urge to perfect the deal by adding complexity. In the end, complexity almost always backfires. Instead, do everything you can to simplify the deal while addressing the critical requirements on both sides of the table.

We'll dive into deal terms later in the book. For now, the takeaway is that in most cases, when designing a startup acquisition, simplicity and efficiency are better than complexity and drag.

Most startups wait far too long before they start developing relationships with PSPs

Magic boxes take a while to understand, and longer to appreciate. Most startups are focused on building their product, raising capital and working with initial customers. They often overlook a fourth critical activity I would recommend adding to the list: developing relationships with relevant PSPs.

This isn't to say you should pour a massive amount of energy into trying to spark near-term business development relationships if they just don't make sense. But you should ensure that the key PSPs in your ecosystem have a developing understanding of the trail you are blazing.

Some commercial opportunities emerge, and that's a bonus. More importantly, it may come to pass that one day the PSP wakes up and has a big idea that your technology might enable. You want to be the first call they make.

Some startups worry about being copied. It happens. But even that can be a mixed blessing. On the downside, if your innovation is easily copied, then it may not be something for which there is ever really going to be an ambient acquisition market. On the upside, if it is hard to build, and a big company went to all the trouble to copy it, then their competitor probably won't want to bother, and is now going to urgently need you!

If they do attempt to copy you, most of them will lack your focus and your degrees of flexibility for trial and error. Most big companies are optimized for efficient execution, and that's about as far culturally from creative exploration as you can get. In order for them to copy you, they would have to copy your entrepreneurial culture—unlikely, easier to buy you.

For many big companies, rapidly iterating on new products is like a rhinoceros trying to climb a tree. If it's a tree they feel they must scale, they'd much prefer to just find a monkey to do it. Be that monkey.

I would argue most startups are better off being "out there," than trying to keep their direction secret. But how do you go about being "out there"?

It's a lot easier than you may think. But before we get down to the tactics, let's be clear on the strategic objective. We're trying to create value.

Chapter 4

Maximizing value

Startup valuation isn't an afterthought or something abstractly constructed by comparing sheets of comparable transactions. Startup valuation is specific to each buyer-seller pairing and is developed from the very start of the relationship with the potential acquirer.

There's only one you

Most of the techniques they teach you in business school don't work when it comes to valuing startups.

Traditional M&A valuation methods look at the financial model of the combined entity, apply some improvements to the model based on various synergies and produce future cash flows. They then calculate the present value of those cash flows, and the buyer and seller arm wrestle over which side has more to do with the reasons that the future cash flows are so attractive.

Finally, they settle on a price that is the mutually-agreed estimate of the seller's contribution to the present value of the said future cash flows.

Startups, however, are typically product-heavy, and have a long way to go to build up their distribution and monetization models. It's very likely that the new innovation will be so deeply embedded in some set of existing acquirer offerings that defining which part of revenue, let alone profit or cash flow, is attributable to the innovation is exceedingly difficult.

Any detailed financial model built to justify a startup acquisition is going to be loaded with so many assumptions and unknowns that it will almost assuredly fall on its face when confronted by any, even junior, financial analyst.

Startup valuation starts with their appreciation of your scarcity

As a thought experiment, let's plot the world of M&A on a graph. On the left side, we'll put three types of acquisitions:

- Metamorphic: Deals that are so substantial, they change or enhance the fundamental nature of the resulting combination
- Transformational: Acquisitions that accelerate the acquirer down an important new path
- Incremental: Combinations that bring operating synergies, but not a great deal more

Along the top of the table, let's describe the key motivator for each kind of acquisition:

- Consolidation: More of what we already do but with a new twist or done more efficiently
- Scarcity: I know I need this and there isn't another one like it out there
- Scale: These guys are big and in combination we can create something, the likes of, the world has never seen

On the next page we see this plotted out.

Acquisition drivers

	Consolidation	Scarcity	Scale
Metamorphic			Powerful market position
Transformational		New technology and expertise	
Incremental	Product overlap and synergies		

On the bottom left, we have traditional acquisitions. These are the kind they love in business school: product overlap with operating synergies. As an example, say your prospective buyer sells ketchup and you sell mustard. You both have a salesperson in Dallas. You both have an expensive head of human resources. Let's bundle the ketchup and mustard into a single pack, fire one salesperson in Dallas and one expensive HR exec. Now calculate the value from this new competitive product bundle and the money saved through streamlined operations. That's the aggregate value of the deal.

On the top right, we have the ability for an acquirer to unlock significant market expansion into an entirely new and important category. Those are acquisitions of companies that have established their position. They got their magic box to the top of the mountain on their own. They have figured out product, distribution and monetization. They are fully formed. Even if they are relatively new, they aren't really startups. Those deals actually kind of work like the ones on the bottom left, but with a lot more zeros.

In the middle is where the startup game is played, and the motivator is scarcity. They are powered by the belief that your startup has new, hard-to-find technology and expertise. But they have to see value in your entire startup. If it's just the people, you'll slip down and to the left into the incremental bucket (a few more talented employees). If it's just the technology, they won't see real value in the direction, just the thing. If you want your startup to be highly valued, they have to believe in what your magic box will yield in the future, that you are the people to unlock its power, and that it is the only one like it in the world.

Everything you do with PSPs should enhance their perception of your technology and your expertise. They have to believe that you are their head start.

Valuation

Valuation is derived from the utility of your startup to a particular buyer and framed by their view of your scarcity.

If the buyer has a billion customers and the addition of your startup means they can make an extra dollar per month from each of them, then in theory the value they'll place on your innovation will be one thousand times greater than a company extracting one dollar per month across a million customers. Naturally, it's never this clean. But you get the idea.

Concurrently, if you're the only way in the world for the buyer to unlock those extra dollars, you're going to be able to claim the credit for a good portion of them. However, if you, along with ten alternative methods, could equally produce the same increased yield, your leverage drops precipitously.

As an aside, it's worth keeping an eye out for the change in behavior that often occurs in startup acquisition discussions. It's a good sign! The conversation about the impact the startup will have on the buyer starts as a pretty open, collaborative exchange of ideas. Maybe a few models are developed, and some spreadsheets go back-and-forth to consider scenarios. Then, suddenly, the topic of value to the buyer abruptly stops. The numbers on their spreadsheets are getting big, and they don't want you to know what you might mean to them. You know you've got them when they no longer want to talk about the numbers but still want to talk about the deal.

The valuation kaleidoscope

There are so many pieces to how the value of a startup is ultimately set that it would be impossible to create a complete list. However, through the countless transactions I've observed, I've seen a few recurring patterns on both the buy and sell sides. Keeping these patterns in mind will help you frame your thinking on valuation and assess the strength of your negotiating position.

Of course, everything would be easier if I could just hand you a looking glass with the power to see into the minds of buyers and sellers. Unfortunately, the best device available is a kaleidoscope that can only show the contours of their assessments and intentions. Fortunately, inside of these continuously transforming images, there are recurring patterns.

On the buyer's side

First, let's think about how this all looks to them. There are going to be any number of opinions on the buy side about the strength of the acquisition thesis. But you'll find that if you can get an understanding (and where possible ahead) of the key areas below, you'll be in pretty good shape for beginning to frame your valuation position. The buy side drivers tend to be:

- Buyer utility
- Capacity to pay
- Sponsorship, focus and urgency
- Cost to own
- Ease of transfer

Let's look at each.

Buyer utility

As we've discussed above, developing a sense of how the buyer views the impact your startup will have on their business is the top priority for developing a feel for what they may be willing to pay to make the acquisition. Sometimes, it's relatively easy to make an estimate of what the potential of the combination may be. Other times, it takes some creative thinking to frame how the resulting economics may work. Naturally, the clearer the framing, the easier it is to develop the valuation framework.

Once you have a frame for the value, the buyer's position will shift to the sharing of the value. They will contend that they are the ones bringing distribution, monetization or another critical ingredient. In their mind, paying for value they are bringing to the table is ludicrous. They will argue that your startup has a value in-and-of-itself and that is the value upon which the transaction should be based. There's some truth in this, but it's not the entire story. Your startup is, in fact, unlocking this value for them, so there should be some sharing of this upside.

If there's no other way for them to unlock this potential other than buying you, then you should be able to claim quite a bit of the value. However, if there are many alternative ways for them to unlock this potential, then there's a good chance they are going to push hard to claim the lion's share.

You have to make a call as to which side is bringing more to the table in order to have a sense of the negotiating cards you have in your hands, and the cards they have in theirs.

Capacity to pay

A potential buyer with an enormous amount of cash and little debt has a great deal more flexibility than one that is levered up and sitting on a matchbox-sized war chest. Or maybe the buyer is trading at an attractive multiple in the public markets and they feel now is a good time to make acquisitions using their highly-valued equity as currency. A buyer's capacity to pay (both real and perceived) will have a significant impact on the way they approach a deal. Once again, it's not about you, it's about them. We will drill down into understanding your potential buyers at the end of this section.

Sponsorship, focus and urgency

The higher up your sponsor is in the organization, the fewer hurdles the acquisition has to clear, and the greater the sway your sponsor has in price and structure. I've seen deals accelerate quickly to a close, after a potential buyer CEO says, "Just get this deal done!" I've also seen a deal die on the spot, when a potential buyer CEO asks, "Why are we doing this again?"

That said, even if the CEO wants to make the acquisition, if other priorities get in the way and the company doesn't have the capacity to focus on the transaction, it can be exceedingly difficult to negotiate or even get the deal done at all. It's important to get a feel for the organizational dynamics across the table. Pushing too hard when the resources simply aren't available on the other side to process the deal (corporate development, legal, etc.) could burn up a lot of goodwill for no gain.

And lastly, if you've gotten to this point you've probably demonstrated some level of scarcity, but does the buyer have a sense of urgency? Is this something the buyer feels they have to do right now? How easily can they postpone this to next year? Can they get what they need in the near-term through a commercial partnership and circle back to discuss something more substantial later? Or do they absolutely, positively, have to own your startup to effect their current priorities?

Cost to own

If you're going to try to understand the full picture of the calculations the buyer is running to determine the full cost of an acquisition, you have to also consider their ongoing cost to own the startup. For starters, most startup teams are working at below-market salaries and will expect to be bumped up to the equivalent pay as their peers in the buyer's organization. As such, the startup's cost structure typically immediately increases upon acquisition. In addition, it can take as long as a couple years to fully integrate the new platform into the buyer's offerings and distribution channels. That can represent significant cost, sometimes on the order of the purchase price itself. If you want to put yourself in the buyer's shoes, you have to consider the cost to acquire the company, the cost to retain the team, the cost to integrate and see benefit from the technology. Only then will you really get a sense of the check the buyer would consider writing to make the acquisition.

Ease of transfer

There are a number of reasons your startup may be difficult to transfer or own post acquisition. Like price dynamics, these transfer dynamics are often quite different from buyer to buyer. For example, maybe you've licensed key elements of your technology from third parties who may or may not be keen on the idea of the company acquiring your startup being an ongoing customer. Or possibly, you've cut a deal with one of your other customers or commercial partners that involves some kind of exclusive relationship. Or maybe the terms you have with a key player in your supply chain work economically at a small scale but, as structured, are cost-prohibitive at a larger scale.

It could even be that your team lives in Antarctica and your buyer will only do the deal if they move to the North Pole. More broadly, your buyer will make their own estimation of the complexities and costs of integrating your startup into their organization.

Post-acquisition integration is a significant undertaking, and can even become the primary factor in the ultimate success or failure of the combination.

Given all of this, simply transferring the company to the new owner may require deals to be cut with, or checks be written to, the various players to get them to go along for the ride. Transfer friction will be priced into the deal one way or another.

On the seller's side

It takes two to tango. What kind of deal do you think you can get done with them? Is now the right time? Are you well positioned to get to a close?

A word to the wise: It's very easy to believe because one buyer is interested in you that many more will be also. Maybe they will. Maybe they won't. Maybe they will, but much farther down the road. I know many entrepreneurs who passed up or goofed up acquisition opportunities that would have been more than sufficient for their needs. They did so as they searched for a bit better of a deal. It's more fun to be in Hawaii thinking about how much you might have been able to get, than to be sitting on the subway thinking about how much fun it would be to be in Hawaii.

That's my warning!

Let's dig in on some of the variables I've seen drive the assessment of a potential acquisition opportunity on the seller's side of the table. Generally speaking, they look like the following:

- Enthusiasm
- Options and constraints
- Assessment of market conditions
- Engagement and momentum
- Talent and likeability

Enthusiasm

These transactions are driven by a combined vision. When you (and by extension your team) are excited about the potential, it shows. When you're not, it also shows.

If, deep down, you don't like the strategy, the culture of the acquirer or the direction you think the transaction will take your career, it will seep through in every interaction with the buyer. Not even stacks of money can overcome a core lack of enthusiasm.

Magic happens when you are enthusiastic. Prepare for meetings, do the extra research, take the extra flight. Spend all day in meetings, and hang out with the buyer well into the night. You are chomping at the bit, and that infects the buyer and gets their team excited as well. Enthusiasm feeds itself and accelerates deals.

Options and constraints

If you have multiple options and feel confident in your ability to negotiate with each potential buyer, you are able to maximize value. This doesn't mean, however, driving an auction and playing buyers off each other. We'll talk about why this can, in many cases, destroy value later in the book. But it does mean having the confidence in your ability to push to find the maximum potential of each combination scenario.

If options are one side of this coin, constraints are the other. The most common constraint for startups is cash. As startups begin to see a significant funding gap on the horizon, their range of options begins to narrow. But funding gaps aren't the only constraint. They may be finding it difficult to retain key team members or that new players are poised to enter their space and dull their competitive edge (making what they do less scarce). Constraints can come in many shapes and sizes.

Assessment of market conditions

It's very hard to time changes in the global financial markets and identify technological and cultural shifts, but you need to have a sense for the macro dynamics in your sector.

Is capital flowing into startups generally like yours or ones with similar business models? Slowing capital flows are a key indicator of market headwinds.

Are companies you would consider relevant to your efforts emerging on the scene, or does it seem like more of the action is around existing market players banding together? If you are going through a period of consolidation, that could mean supply exceeds demand and it may take time for the market to catch up.

Are customers starting to pull back on expenditures? If you're seeing reduced demand or downward pricing pressure, how is your business plan impacted?

Any, and all, of these should elevate your thinking around finding yourself supported by a larger balance sheet.

Engagement and momentum

When you're raising expansion capital, topline growth is critical (at least in customer acquisition, and hopefully in both customer acquisition and revenue), and for good reason. Expansion-phase investment is ultimately a bet on demand, and is typically going toward distribution (customer acquisition). If a startup is hard pressed to show significant customer demand from relatively accessible customers, there's a good chance the expansion capital will be used inefficiently and the company will squander the money without seeing the commensurate growth.

Things are a bit different for PSPs. They probably have distribution and can get the product into the market. More likely than not, their biggest concern is not accessing new customers but increasingly captivating the ones they have. That customers like theirs see tremendous value from, and are highly engaged with, the platform (in whatever form such engagement is appropriately measured) is the positive signal they're looking for.

Momentum, in this case, isn't necessarily topline revenue or user growth. Momentum comes in different forms, and can be showcased in a number of ways: increasing usage, growth inside of existing customers, volume of transactions and so on. All of these can show the kind of momentum (increasing value and greater engagement) in which the buyer is keenly interested.

The definition of “momentum” becomes a key consideration when a startup is approaching a funding gap. There will be pressure from some constituents to do everything possible to drive topline growth in order to attract the next round of capital. Other constituents may be more keen to conserve cash and seek to throttle back expenditure, maximize runway and be positioned to be acquired.

There’s no single solution for relieving this tension. There are cases where either strategy can make sense. But, as it relates to PSPs, there are many cases where topline growth in-and-of-itself won’t be their primary concern, and a strategy that extends your runway and enables you to show improving “case study” level metrics is one you should seriously consider. PSPs and VCs use different measuring sticks and have different priorities. But PSPs move slowly, so the more time you have the better.

Said differently, optimizing for scale and optimizing for sale can be quite different from each other.

Talent and likeability

How good is your team, really? If you put your team up against the top people at the biggest tech giants, would they outshine, hang in there or struggle to keep up? Your assessment of your team is a critical consideration as you evaluate acquisition opportunities.

Your team will face a great deal of scrutiny in any acquisition process. This scrutiny can be intense, particularly from companies with sophisticated teams operating in areas similar to your startup. If you have a deal on the table and you pass it up because you believe there may be a chance down the line that a much larger deal could be achieved with a more sophisticated buyer, you had better be sure your team is the best in the world.

The last piece of the puzzle is likeability. Are you and your team people with whom the buyer is going to enjoy working? Does it feel like a comfortable fit when everyone is together? Likeability and fit are tough ones to define, but, as the saying goes, you know them when you see them.

I've seen people make crazy demands or say exactly the wrong thing, at the eleventh hour causing a deal to evaporate in an instant. Remember: Confidence is inspiring; humility is endearing; arrogance is a deal killer.

Know your buyers

We're going to take a short detour through your likely buyer types. It's important to have a sense of who is sitting across the table from you, and what to expect from different types of acquirers as you anticipate how acquisition scenarios may unfold.

In broad strokes, let's divide buyers into five groupings:

- Technology giants
- Established corporations
- Small public companies
- High-growth private companies
- Private equity

Naturally, there are all kinds of variations on these themes, but these five should give you a pretty good overview.

Technology giants

These companies understand magic boxes. They know how to acquire startups. For companies they want, they are often flexible on valuation. However, quite often they believe whatever technology the startup has developed won't work at their scale, in their environment or is in black and white and they want color. As such, their interest can lean toward the team, and convincing them of the value in the overall platform (and not just the talent) can be a challenging proposition. A home run is when they see value in the platform. A double is when they see value in the expertise of the team as a unified unit. You can sometimes knock a single if they see value in just the individuals on the team, even if they plan to split them up and distribute them across their organization.

Established corporations

Established corporations who have historically only made acquisitions of companies similar to themselves, and based on relative rates of profitability, are challenging buyers of startups. They weren't born of a magic box (or at least not as far as anyone can remember). Placing big bets on still-to-be-proven ideas is not typically how they roll. Their deal teams are used to valuing businesses based on operating profits, and their heads spin and sometimes explode when they have to consider how to value a business that is still consuming, rather than generating, cash.

These organizations will occasionally hire a head of innovation and make some effort to engage with startups. But normally, these new executives are ministers without portfolio, and when the time comes to get a deal done, they find the rest of the organization has disappeared behind them. If you don't have a very senior executive (like the CEO, head of the business unit or an exceedingly well-positioned R&D executive) personally driving the deal on the buy side, the likelihood of the deal getting done is probably pretty low.

That said, there is a good side to these companies in that you are bringing to them something they don't already have. Because of that, when all the stars align, valuations can sometimes be even more attractive than the ones you'd receive from tech giants who already have lots of people just like you walking the halls. To established corporations, you are a rare creature with powers to wield new and magical forces.

Small public companies

If tech giants are lions, established corporations are rhinoceroses, startups are monkeys, then small public companies are lemurs. Many of them have magic-box DNA and think like startups. However, quite often they are right on the edge of profitability (a bit over or a bit under). They are highly sensitive to anything that is going to nudge their income statement the wrong way (as the market is intensely focused on their short-term performance). As such, this group of buyers can be a bit shy.

If you are going to be financially accretive (you're already profitable), then the conversation gets easier. If you can develop a very clear strategy for how you can get profitable pretty quickly with them, there's probably some kind of story to be had. But if you are still going to be consuming resources for a while to come, even if they have the money on the balance sheet (or strong currency in their equity), the hurdle for an acquisition will be quite high. Not to say impossible, as they will probably have good startup genes, but quite high as they are very likely focused on their near-term financial profile. They have to be.

High-growth private companies

If it wasn't for the fact that they almost always want you to take their stock as payment, this would be the ideal startup buyer group. These companies are on their way to getting their magic box to the top of the mountain. They have the plan. They have the resources. They are on the move.

But they aren't there yet. They know there are still ravines over which they will need to build bridges, and you might be a useful construction set. However, everything about them is focused on the mission. All their resources and energies are directed toward getting to the top of the mountain. If you want to join forces, it's going to take belief in their vision. There will likely be some receptivity to your need to take some money off the table. But in most cases, they will offer to swap your equity for theirs. There are ways to mitigate the risks of largely equity deals. But ultimately, deals with this group are about combining forces to reach the summit.

Private equity

For the most part, this isn't a great startup buyer category. Private equity folks are typically focused on businesses that they can incrementally improve and predictably grow. They'd prefer to roll up all the Popsicle sellers on the beach under a single brand, cut half of them, increase prices and maybe acquire an iced tea company, since they already have the cart space.

On occasion, they will see the need for your startup as part of one of their portfolio companies. To this end, they can be worth a call to bounce ideas around. But for the most part, this is a longer-shot path.

With this tour through our target buyer types completed, we understand who to call, and what to expect from each. But what are we going to say?

Time to tell our story.

Chapter 5

Narrative

Presenting your magic box in a way that leads to the creation of the big idea isn't as hard as you may think.

Your presentation should start a conversation

This chapter outlines the way to organize your presentation for PSPs. If all you do is follow this outline, you'll be heading in the right direction, and of course, there are any number of ways to customize and improve on this approach. What I'm most interested in is the general flow. How you present the material is your call.

What you are trying to do is paint a picture of the way the world is moving and show how your current offerings are a manifestation of your understanding of the broader shifts in the market.

But it also needs to have a tangible feel. If the presentation is too abstract you will lose the audience. In addition, as we discussed in the section on the big idea, the presentation should create a conversation and open the door to the discussion of how your startup fits with their strategy. So, having all the answers isn't the objective, creating a dialogue is.

Each of the following sections could be a single slide, or a series of slides but keep the conceptual flow. I've found this ordering fosters discussion while also delivering a great deal of information in a digestible form.

Here is the complete list before we dive in on the content for each:

- Mission
- Problem/opportunity statement
- Solution statement
- Key elements of approach
- Platform
- Strengths
- Key metrics
- Unit economics
- User praise
- Media recognition
- Market size

- Market drivers
- Competitive advantages
- Case studies
- Core competencies
- Deep dive
- Technology stack
- Platform components
- Intellectual property
- Team
- Company status

You may be thinking "blah, blah, blah, I already know how to create a presentation." I'm sure you do, but trust me, this flow will greatly help the articulation of your value, showcase your scarcity and increase your chances of catalyzing the buyer's big idea. It's important to get this right, and that's why I'm including all this detail. Let's get going.

Mission

Starting with a simple and tangible mission statement is very helpful in framing the conversation. It should be directional about the role your startup is looking to play in the market. You also want it to be action oriented, so I normally recommend starting with some form of "to be the..."

The mission for Advsr Ideas might be "to be the premier provider of strategic insights for startups." That mission may seem broad, but it's safer to risk being too broad, than too narrow. This mission sets up a number of good questions: What are "strategic insights"? How do you define "startups"? What does it mean to be "premier" (why not say "biggest")? Why not say "publisher" instead of "provider"?

This mission opens the door for us to discuss the global explosion in entrepreneurship, and how the cost to start a company has come way down, and how most kids in college aren't planning on getting a regular job and so on.

This book is just the current manifestation of Advsr Ideas' vision. There may be a website, a mobile app, a TV series and a feature-length movie—all pouring wisdom into the unquenchable thirst of an entrepreneurial mind. I'm getting fired up!

What you want is the mission to get the receiver to lean in and ask, "What do you mean by that?"

Problem/opportunity statement

This is a statement that sets up the broad problem to be solved or the opportunity to be captured. It shouldn't be more than a handful of key points that are irrefutable. You want heads to nod. A few illustrations or a picture or two can go a long way on this slide.

Solution statement

The slide should essentially articulate how your company is going to address the challenges raised in the previous slide. This slide should align with the mission statement. It should also speak directly to what the company is developing today and provide context for the offerings being rolled out in the future.

Key elements of approach

These are the building blocks of the new platform ("platform" being my catch-all term for the innovation you're developing). This is the "hard things we've solved" part of the presentation. It's going to showcase the sophistication of your approach and the hurdles one would have to overcome to develop solutions in this category. This slide done well should inspire the recipients to realize they aren't well positioned to create these kinds of innovations, or even better, that they needed these capabilities yesterday.

Platform

Up to this point, the presentation has been pretty high level and abstract. It's time to give the receiver a sense of the platform itself. If the platform is a chip, a molecule or something difficult to visualize, then show a conceptual overview of the innovation. The point here is you want to make it real. Give them something on which to hang their hats.

For many types of startups, this slide is a summary of features on one side and a few screen shots on the other. Make sure whatever images you use are easy to see. It's better to have one clear image than three small or grainy ones.

Strengths

It's time to articulate the power of the innovation. Lay out the strengths of the platform. Think broadly about what this new approach enables and for whom it enables it. How does it change the world? What super power does it possess? What can be done now that couldn't be done before? In short, how has your innovation made the process ten times or hundred times better than alternative methods?

Key metrics

Illustrate how this new innovation is being adopted, making a difference or creating value. These are not financial metrics. Rather metrics around usage, consumption and engagement. If there aren't broad metrics, then show case studies or examples that illustrate a pattern of adoption. PSPs typically care more about quality than quantity. Show that this thing, when in the right hands, really works.

Unit economics

Not only is the offering being adopted but the underlying unit economics are strong. As with the key metrics slide, focus more on gross profit (revenue minus cost of goods sold), customer lifetime value (profit realized during a customer's time with you) and other key drivers of long-term success than on aggregate financial performance. In particular, if the unit economics improve dramatically at larger scales, make sure to make that point. Along these lines, you can create a table showing how your unit economics improve at increasingly large scales. This form of presentation can be very effective in sparking a conversation around how fast your startup could grow in collaboration with the PSP.

In most cases, they are going to be bringing the customers with you bringing the product. In cases where that is reversed, articulate how your platform will reduce the cost of customer acquisition or bring valuable reach. For example, if you've done a great job building a channel into a specific market, or attracting a valuable audience, think about what others are spending to reach the same people, and begin to frame the value of your channel.

This is different from your VC pitch, where you have to nail all three key strategy elements: product, distribution and monetization. In this presentation, you want to lean toward your strengths, and then work with the PSP to fill in the rest. In short, you want a discussion to erupt about how together your combined unit economics are improved and intriguing.

User praise

Now we want to showcase what users say about the platform. In particular, highlight quotes illustrating something specific about your customers' use of the platform and value they've derived. Bold parts of the quote if they are on the longer side. Fit three to five quotes (more will probably get lost on the screen). The voice of the customer is powerful and often forgotten in presentations.

Media recognition

Showcase media mentions and any awards. Again, look for quotes that speak to the strength of the innovation, and more broadly, its impact on the market. If you have a large number of press mentions, pick the top three to five and showcase them in the top three quarters of the page, and then have the logos of the notable publications along the bottom of the page. Third-party validation boosts your perception as a market leader.

Market size

This can be pretty high level, and should showcase the macro scale of the broad market sectors in which the startup operates. Typically, three to five bullet points on one side of the page, and one or two graphs/charts on the other side of the page are sufficient to tell the story. It's probably the case that the PSP isn't going after the market in exactly the same way you are, so specific numbers of the exact sizes of addressable markets are probably not critical. If they are going after a similar market, there's also a good chance that they know more about it than you!

Market drivers

This slide tends to get entrepreneurs up on their soapboxes. It's positioned deep into the deck to keep you from overpowering the conversation early on. What you want here is an overview of trends in the favor of your startup's direction. These can be quite broad strokes, like increasing disintermediation of certain market players or increasing consumer expectations around availability or ease of use and so on. They can also drill down into specific market or regulatory dynamics. This slide describes the cultural, technological and economic shifts creating the market opportunity into which you are endeavoring.

Competitive advantages

This slide brings it all home: A table showing your approach versus alternate ways of solving the problem. Avoid making this a "feature comparison" versus directly competitive platforms (they might be the folks in the room!). Instead, focus more broadly on the strengths and weaknesses of alternate ways of approaching the problem: The alternates down the left side and key attributes across the top, your company and three-or-so alternatives, with four or five attributes. Score each alternative for each attribute (could be as simple as an up arrow or a down arrow). An example for Advsr Ideas:

Sources of strategic insights for startups

	Magic box enabled	Startup-specific	Readily available	Low cost
Advsr Ideas	+	+	+	+
Small business books	-	-	+	+
Investment bankers	-	+	-	-

Case studies

Provide one, two or three case studies—one per slide or all together on one slide. Focus on how the customer used the platform and the value they received. Very often startups don't have huge commercial scale. But they do have depth and engagement with certain types of customers. Case studies provide a powerful way to show how the platform works in the real world. Remember, people think in narrative. The case studies are the narrative of your platform.

Core competencies

You need the PSP to appreciate not only the strength of your platform but also the strength of your team. They need to realize they won't be able just to hire a few folks to knock this out, but that your team represents a hard-to-assemble collection of skills and talents. Before you dive in on your platform, you'll want to take a moment to showcase the skillsets required to develop this technology. This slide should highlight three to five key core competencies of your team (not features of the platform—rather skills of the team). So for example they could be: big data, analytics, genomics, user experience, mobile, marketplaces, social media, physics engines, enterprise security, whatever makes your team special. What are the hard-to-find skillsets required to pull off this new innovation? Showcase your team's areas of deep expertise.

Deep dive

Features, capabilities, pictures, even links to videos—what do you want to showcase about the platform? This can be one to ten slides and can go into as much detail as needed around key capabilities. It can also include a product roadmap if you think it would help show your direction. But understand: Your product roadmap in their hands will very likely look quite different from the roadmap you've imagined for yourself. Don't come off too wedded to a single path forward. Instead, showcase open-ended opportunities for future enhancements or products, opportunities that might comport nicely with the direction the market is going and the PSP's aspirations.

Technology stack

In virtually every meaningful meeting, you will be asked about the technologies in which you develop. Have this slide ready to go. Everyone will like it!

Platform components

You'll want to showcase the depth of the platform and its complexity—both to demonstrate the hard work that's gone into it and to show how hard it would be for someone else to build something similar.

Have a slide offering a broad overview of the platform, with "big blocks" representing its "core working elements." Have a second slide (or set of slides) that "explodes" the bigger blocks into smaller constituent elements. Product anatomy is very helpful.

If relevant, also have a slide showing connections to third-party services such as security, payments or other key integration partners. For nondigital businesses, this may be logistics enablers, production processes or relationships with suppliers. Don't be shy about articulating how difficult it was to create the entire ecosystem in which your innovation exists.

Intellectual property

If you have pending or granted patents, summarize them. It's also fine to discuss key pieces of hard-to-develop, or hard-to-duplicate, technology in this section. You can also include any other assets of note, like effective domain names, trademarks and so on. If you don't have anything substantial IP-wise, just omit this slide and focus on the processes you've improved and the applied nature of your platform.

Team

Presentations oriented toward venture capital investors normally highlight the team early on. "First, people; then, market; then, product" is the usual ordering of priorities for many VCs. However, as it relates to PSPs, your team shines brightest after the entire body of work has been articulated, hence why it's this far back in this presentation. Talk about your team in relation to an entire story of accomplishment. Use this part of your presentation to flesh out the breadth and depth of all that's been achieved and all the brilliant work that went into achieving it. Typically, the team slide has a summary of the key management team members on one side and then a summary of the overall organization on another. No need to list every person.

Company status

This slide should summarize what has been accomplished to date and outline a few of the "big picture" components of your growth strategy (e.g., we need to expand distribution or enter new markets). This slide should open the floor to a discussion about how much faster you could grow if you joined forces. Include some bullet points on key company specs (year founded, locations, amount of capital raised to date, notable investors, etc.). These specs will gently move the conversation toward you as an entity. One that could, hmm, be acquired.

A few more thoughts on the narrative

The venue for all of this content is a presentation that is typically twenty-five to thirty-five slides in length. You won't typically present every slide in every meeting with a PSP, but you will want to have them all readily available.

In addition to this core presentation, you'll frequently find that you'll have insights into the opportunities created in combination with a specific PSP. Incorporating these evolving ideas can be powerful, particularly if the PSP's team is actively involved in the brainstorming. Start to have your presentation reflect their collaboration, and more importantly, their big idea.

What's not in this deck

Typically, you're not going to want to include detailed financial projections in an initial discussion with PSPs. Nor do you want to dive into your startup's financial history at this point. Keep the conversation high level and for goodness' sake don't end your presentation with everyone's nose buried in spreadsheets. You want them reaching for their telescopes, not their microscopes.

What to share when

Typically, I wouldn't circulate the entire presentation without having a nondisclosure agreement ("NDA") in place. Normally, I would suggest using the first few slides as an introductory deck, one that can be shared with pretty much anyone in advance of an NDA. If there's interest in having a deep-dive conference call, it's probably fine to present (but not send) the full presentation (removing any particularly sensitive parts). Only distribute the full presentation if the conversation elevates to the point of putting in place an NDA.

Financial supplement

Once you have an NDA in place, you're going to pretty quickly get a request from the PSP for financial information. It's good to have a short presentation handy that summarizes your recent performance—previous year and current year income statement and a current balance sheet are probably enough at this stage. I also find it helpful to share a summary capitalization table. Naturally, you don't have to share all this information. But if you believe this is a legitimate opportunity and you're genuinely trying to move the conversation forward, it's best to just tell it like it is right out of the gate.

Important point: Your current financial profile is mostly likely not why they are interested in you, so also include with your financial summary an overview of what your startup does and a few key nonfinancial metrics (slides from your narrative deck like strengths, key metrics and unit economics—and if you really want to go for it—user praise). The reason is that the financial supplement is quite often forwarded to finance folks who have very little context to work with. If all they receive is a summary of some pretty uninspiring financials, then they're probably not going to react very favorably. On the other hand, if they receive a deck showing great things happening, they may embrace a more positive view of the new platform and its prospects. Taking this one step further, if you feel like you have a handle on the combined opportunity, it could help your case to include an outline of the potential economics of the combination. Finance people hate losing money, but they love a sound investment—showcase that you are the latter!

Team and platform supplement

Similarly, though normally a bit farther down the line, you will likely also receive requests for deeper information on the team. Don't just ship them a pile of resumes and online profiles that fail to present your team in any kind of context. Prepare a supplemental presentation highlighting the core competencies, platform elements and technology environments described in your long-form presentation. Add in any discussion you feel is appropriate to showcase the team's remarkable talents and experience. Then provide more detail on key individuals and contributors.

Data room

Your "data room" is the archive of all the info you're going to need to complete the deal. Start preparing your data room early. For reasons I'll get into later, the data room isn't just the product of a set of annoying boxes to be checked. It plays a pivotal role in your negotiating strategy and will (quite likely) figure heavily in the terms of the deal you ultimately complete. The data room is important and it takes time to build, particularly if you've used a number of third-party consultants, law firms and other service providers. Just the act of collecting important documents can take weeks, or even months.

Your attorneys can give you a data room checklist. Focus on key items like corporate formation, capitalization, material agreements (with customers and suppliers), and employment matters. A typical startup's data room will contain hundreds of documents. If you review your current data room and it's only a dozen documents, then you're nowhere close to where you're going to need to be. Be well prepared for a good deal and you'll increase your chances of actually getting one!

Chapter 6

Thought leadership

How do I use all this stuff?

You need to have an air game

If directly reaching out to potential PSPs is your ground game, then thought leadership is your air game. And just as in football, the air game requires a bit more finesse from the quarterback. The air game isn't simply a matter of putting your head down and plowing forward.

You need to demonstrate your ability to see the entire field and predict how plays will unfold. Show that you're out in front of the various forces at work and able to foresee developing circumstances.

Fostering your startup's acquisition opportunities is easier when you're recognized by opinion leaders in your domain as a framer, and possibly even a shaper, of the market's future opportunities.

You should have intellectual traction with key observers of your theater of enterprise. Mind you, you're not giving away all the proprietary thinking you've developed in the process. Instead, you're positioning yourself as a visionary and articulator of the market's directions and opportunities. To put it another way, when key players in this arena think about the market's evolutionary directions, your name comes to mind in an intelligently positive way.

By framing, I mean talking about the direction, the challenges and the opportunities in your market. You don't need to tie these directly to the offerings of your startup. It's more a matter of how you view the market unfolding at a macro level and the opportunities and challenges you see in your image of this future.

If opinion leaders, influencers and decision makers see you as having a robust and insightful vision of the future, they'll seek you out. That's powerful.

Now here's a twist—that corps of relevant opinion leaders, influencers and decision makers may be a very small set of people. Maybe even only one key player! Establishing yourself may not be about posting ten items per day on social media, writing a blog or penning a white paper. Your strategy may consist of five-minute presentations at conferences, phone conversations or e-mails that capture the essence of a topic.

How to go about establishing yourself as a thought leader is highly contextual and will also be largely dependent on your own personality. Still, establishing your place in the arena will be key. It's a process. It takes time and creativity but shouldn't be overlooked. It makes you relevant.

Maybe you're one of those ultra-stealthy founders who just doesn't want to reveal anything to anybody. That's fine. But understand that the downside of that approach is that few PSPs will know anything about you. Your reticence is setting you up to have to make the entire trek up the mountain on your own. If a time comes when the trek turns treacherous or simply too slow, you're going to want to develop acquisition interest in your company. And since no one knows about you, you may find yourself alone on the mountain.

Developing acquisition interest takes time. Give yourself time to build awareness and develop relationships.

The genuine article

The beauty of not being a recluse and instead being "in the industry conversation" is that doing so authenticates you. You may be right some of the time and wrong most of the time, but if you approach the dialogue with an open mind it won't matter. And the benefits of being "out there" are enormous.

For instance, I always precirculate a piece I'm writing to one or two people whose opinions I value. Being "out there" can be as simple as doing things like that. Even relatively senior and influential (and busy!) people are almost always happy to have a quick sidebar to share their feedback and perspectives. Reaching out to collaborate around shared experience is a great tool. And the product of these conversations, be it a piece of writing, a slide in a presentation or even a single observation is usually something of interest more broadly in the industry. Everybody benefits.

Getting started

It's entirely your call as to how you want to establish yourself as a thought leader. You may prefer a narrow, highly targeted strategy or maybe you'll feel more comfortable shouting your message from the mountain tops!

Where to start

In building your rep, build on the broad themes of the PSP-focused presentation we developed in the previous chapter. In the context of your mission and the direction of the market, discuss the sector's shifting ground. Take the market drivers you outlined in your presentation and make each the topic of a blog post. Reach out to a few key industry leaders. You'll find that a few hundred words will fall onto the page almost by themselves. And most folks aren't going to read much more than that anyway! I'll wager that you'll also learn something of value for your startup and strategy in the process.

Delivery

Short-form social media are a great way to be in front of people and for them to get to know your personality. But they're not a venue for thoughtful commentary. One-line pontifications layered over a shared post are not going to cut it. They can be used here and there to make (or follow up on) a specific point, but they just aren't adequate to the task of conveying original and fully elaborated ideas.

I would say the minimum buy-in for entry into the thought leadership arena is your own blog. I've used video and audio. But the most mileage comes from short, thoughtfully written blog posts. They become second nature to create; they shouldn't take much time to produce; and they have a nice, long shelf life. If you want to take things to the next level, blend in some video. The hurdles for creating compelling video content have been so greatly lowered that virtually anyone can film a segment or hold an interview from virtually any device. Start with text, but once you have things rolling, consider experimenting with video.

Knock out a few posts discussing key market drivers. Just don't make the mistake of starting and then letting it trail off. Make it a steady priority—put it in your calendar. Before you know it, you'll be viewed as a seer!

Befriend the media

Media outlets are always looking for fresh perspectives and new voices. Journalists are constantly looking to bounce around ideas and are thirsty for data. When probed for insight, be pithy; speak in sound bites; be provocative; and, if warranted, even hyperbolic. Journalists love nothing more than juicy headlines and controversy. They will stay close to anyone who can give them that. Develop a cult of personality around you and your startup.

Event organizers are on a continuous search for speakers and panelists. Don't just identify the media sources your targets read and the industry-related events in which they participate. Identify specific people in industry-related organizations who can help deliver your message. Offer to help them out by contributing a piece to their publication or filling in at an event. Even volunteering will get you in the door to an event, and, if you're enterprising and charismatic could keep that door open. There are many ways to develop relationships in the industry. Make use of them.

There are probably only a few directly relevant media organizations in relation to your startup. At each, moreover, only one or two people will be relevant to your efforts. So building relationships with media may not be as big a job as it may seem at first.

What's more, you'll soon discover media people are well connected in your sector. Hence, building relationships with media may generate a nice multiplier effect down the road. They often are clearinghouses of the key influencers in your industry. Find your way into those circles and create your own luck.

Chapter 7

The ground game

This feels like work

You understand your magic box. Your mind is open to all the possible ways your innovation could be commercialized. You appreciate how long these relationships can take to develop. You know your target PSPs and you're ready to develop their appreciation for your innovation. You've begun to establish yourself as a thought leader.

All systems are go. Now what?

Make a list

There can be anywhere from a few dozen to a few hundred PSPs for a startup. Make as extensive a list of PSPs as you can. Organize by sector. Score by where you feel your startup could add the most value. Identify where you and your stakeholders have strong existing relationships and where you need to start developing them. Some may be candidates for commercial partnerships, others may only be relevant as acquirers; regardless, take time to learn about all of them.

You may not end up approaching all or even most of the targets on your list but having them identified will force you to periodically reevaluate the potential of a relationship with them. Read their press releases. Identify their key players. Before you know it, you'll know a great deal about them.

Include PSPs in adjacent markets. Even though they may not be operating in your sector today, they may decide to enter down the road, and you'll be ready to become relevant to their efforts.

Process phases

Let's structure the way we approach targets into three phases:

- Phase 1—Awareness
- Phase 2—Relationships
- Phase 3—Activation

These three phases are both the framework for your approach across all targets generally as well as the way you will likely see your relationship with each target develop specifically.

Phase 1: Awareness

During this phase, reach out to target PSPs looking for opportunities for collaboration. The approach can be open ended and high level. The outreach can originate directly from you, or via one of your board members, investors or advisors. Often the ideal entry point in the organization is the executive in charge of the product strategy for products relevant to yours.

The art in this phase is identifying the right person and finding a way to get your story in front of them in such a way that it will receive a thoughtful hearing. The good news is that the right person should be quite receptive to learning about an innovative new company in a field in which they've got a real stake. Once you find that person, in most cases, the conversation shouldn't be too difficult to initiate.

What to do once you have their attention?

One of your advisors has introduced you to the right person at one of your top targets. What do you do? Ask to go out for a coffee? Have a quick phone call?

In these situations, I'm a fan of both structure and efficiency. When you grab a cup of coffee or have a short phone call, the power of your idea can be lost in pleasant chit-chat. What seemed like a good opportunity can drift away into irrelevance. You've been formally introduced to an important person in your arena, possibly one of the most important. Don't squander the opportunity on a cup of coffee and idle chatter.

With venture capital investors, the norm is an in-person meeting. Venture capital firms are typically small organizations with tight-knit decision makers. So it's easy to get everyone who needs to hear your story into one room. For PSPs, on the other hand, the people relevant to your startup may be distributed across the far-flung globe.

For first contacts with PSPs, therefore, I've found the best first-meeting venue is a web conference. It's an easy medium. They can invite anybody from their organization they wish, and you won't get bogged down in the sometimes cumbersome logistics of physical meetings.

Now, you can present your complete narrative in a structured and clear way to a handpicked group pulled together by your initial contact.

On a logistical note, make sure everything works. Don't have someone else on your team send the calendar invite. Then a third person set up the web conference and possibly distribute the wrong conference call line. Then struggle with how to share your screen, only to have your instant messenger suddenly pop up with a message about the party tomorrow night. Poorly planned web conferences frequently have bumpy starts and technical glitches. Use a generally available platform, one with which you are proficient!

Get the environment set perfectly. Practice the entire flow from sending the invitation through to closing it all down when the meeting is finished. Ask for feedback and make adjustments. If you have a demo, have it loaded and have your demo data prepopulated. Make sure your voice is clear to the audience (avoid using a speakerphone). Having things go smoothly will reflect well on you. Having them go badly doesn't.

Managing the web conference

For these meetings, I recommend a quick round of introductions of your group (no need to give your life story, just a few career highlights). Then ask the organizer if they could give a quick overview of their group, what piqued their interest in your startup and if there are specific areas they would like you to cover.

In most books on selling stuff, they recommend that you start meetings by asking lots of questions. This enables you to develop an understanding of the needs of the potential customer and fit your offering into them. The risk of that approach in web conferences is that your fifteen minutes asking them questions about their business may erode their interest (they already know about themselves). You'll slowly start to hear keyboards clicking as the participants begin to check their e-mail. They are attending to learn about you: Get to the good stuff pretty quickly.

Handle the deep dive about them in a separate call with the organizer (either in follow up, or if it seems more appropriate, in advance of the web meeting with the larger team).

Make sure they know that you would like to keep the meeting conversational and that they are more than welcome to stop and ask questions as you go. Discussion is something to encourage, not to fear. It means ideas are emerging and taking shape. Disagreements are gold. Don't shut them down. Instead, tease them out. You want your meeting's participants to be engaged, thinking, arguing. You're talking about a new idea. It may run counter to things they hold dear.

However, keep the conversation in sync with your narrative. Try not to skip around too much as that will chop up the story, and you won't paint the full picture. The trick is to keep the discussion lively and on track at the same time.

One in five

Sometimes PSPs will already be considering paths that considerably overlap with your startup's intended direction. In my experience, there's roughly a 20 percent chance of that happening. This doesn't mean the PSP has an acquisition thesis completely formed. But it's a good indicator that you're working on something that is relevant to the bigger players in your space.

The flip side of this 20 percent rule of thumb is the 80 percent chance that the relevant PSPs haven't been contemplating the market opportunity your startup is pursuing. Startups tend to be well ahead of the PSPs in their industry, sometimes years ahead. That's why they are startups!

Simply because you don't have PSPs falling over themselves to acquire you upon their first introduction doesn't mean they won't, in time, come to appreciate the trail you are blazing. It just means their appreciation of your innovation is going to have a longer gestation period.

Death is just the beginning

Right now, your job is to get on their radar. They may slam the door in your face five times before they wake up one morning and realize the thing you've been telling them for years has in fact turned into reality. Around half of the deals I've seen completed have been with a group that had previously passed on the opportunity. Somewhere deep down, your idea will finally take hold, and in time, they will come back around. This isn't the outlier. This is the norm. Rejoice in rejection! It means they paid attention to you, and now you're on their mind.

Phase 2: Relationships

Once you've had an opportunity to introduce yourself to the key companies on your target list, the next phase is developing the relationship. This may be as simple as periodic pings with updates on progress or ideas for collaboration. This is a great place to integrate your thought-leadership strategy with your business development efforts. Create opportunities to have conversations with key players at important PSPs. A report, or a blog post, or something you plan to discuss at an upcoming conference can be the reason for a call to a general manager or a product head at a PSP.

Beyond high-level conversations, there may be opportunities for commercial partnerships. Even small commercial relationships can create important dependencies on your platform. These dependencies can help create momentum toward acquisition, both from the PSP in question, other suppliers to that PSP, and possibly even the PSP's competitors.

If you do get a commercial partnership up and running, don't miss opportunities to share good news or interesting discoveries with the key executives at the PSP (in this case, the Potential Strategic Partner is no longer "potential," so technically now becoming an "SP," but we'll keep calling them PSP to keep everyone from getting dizzy from acronyms!). Once the operating teams are connected, it's easy to move on to other pressing matters in your organization. Don't lose sight of the fact that companies with whom you already have deep commercial relationships are your most likely acquirers. Stay close to them, use every opportunity to build value in their eyes.

In your ongoing conversations with the PSP, don't simply focus the dialogue on what you can do today. Keep a "where can we go from here?" thread in every conversation. Remind them of the potential scale of the opportunities you could unlock together.

This middle phase is where the best stuff happens

In my experience, the best acquisition prospects have emerged from Phase 2.

When you get a “hit” during your initial outreach in Phase 1, it’s typically a partial match. There’s excitement from the buyer about this new idea, but there are also pieces that don’t quite align. A way is found to make it all work, but the combination has rough edges.

When you move into Phase 3, which we’ll get into next, you’re often relying more on loss aversion rather than excitement around maximizing the opportunity. Again, it’s not the perfect set of dynamics.

Phase 2 is when things are ideal. The inbound buyer has had time to consider what you do, has developed a clear strategy and a deep thesis—a thesis that features you. The stars are aligned and there is strong commitment across the buyer’s organization to making the acquisition. All systems are go.

The best deals are done when the buyer is coming to you with everything figured out on their end. The challenge is you just don’t know how long that will take. It can be weeks. It can be years.

Phase 3: Activation

Up to now, I've stressed that startup acquisitions represent the start of a combined journey to the top of the mountain, and that the idea of taking the trek needs to originate from the buyer.

Yet there comes a time when you either want, or need, to press the issue. It may be that some of your team's members are looking for bigger paychecks, there's a looming funding gap or rising competitive pressures are at hand—lots of possible reasons.

The good news is that you've followed all the steps in this book! You've positioned yourself as a thought leader. You've had collaborative open-ended conversations with the key players at your top PSPs. You've developed a set of impressive commercial relationships and dependencies. You've inspired a number of theses around how you and your PSPs could combine to build value in the future.

What you're not is an unknown company, rushing in the door with a newfangled widget, trying to get a deal done overnight.

Loss aversion

The reality of the activation phase is that you're playing more on loss aversion than opportunity maximization.

In Phase 2, when a PSP has a fully formed thesis and is coming inbound to make an enabling acquisition, you are well positioned to realize maximum value.

In Phase 3, you're employing their disinclination to see you acquired by someone else, or worse, by a direct competitor. In that case, of course, they'd miss out on the opportunities your startup harbors. And those opportunities may flow to somebody else. Worse still, they may have developed a dependency on you, so that your departure will cause them the pain and inconvenience of finding a replacement. You're counting on their aversion to losing you.

You can get deals done in Phase 3, but loss aversion doesn't typically drive the same kind of valuation as opportunity maximization does in Phase 2.

But, for whatever reason, you're on a short track. Here's the playbook:

Prioritize

We covered preparation in the last chapter. If you're going into activation mode, make sure you have everything at your fingertips. Events can unfold quickly. You have to be in front of, and not behind, the action. Have your presentation, supplemental materials and data room all ready to roll.

You're looking for two to four concurrently interested potential buyers. That's about all you'll be able to support simultaneously when you factor in meetings, due diligence and so on.

To this end, let's sort your targets into three buckets. In the first bucket are your top candidates: The ones you believe have a clear need, the ones with whom you've created deep relationships, the ones who only need a nudge.

In the second bucket are the ones you're probably going to punt. These are folks like direct competitors who may make sense in extreme situations but also represent a great deal of risk. You're going to put these folks on hold for now. You can decide how to handle them later (if at all).

In the third bucket is everyone else. This group is going to be handled in bulk, and it's going to be largely up to them to raise their hand and show interest. There's only so much you can do to compel folks to move quickly. It's most likely that the top ten to twenty in your first bucket are the ones who are going to see the need for you, and act. Don't overinvest in the PSPs in bucket three. The activation phase takes an enormous amount of effort in a short period of time. You have to carefully place your bets, and the folks in bucket three are long shots.

Avoid jiggery-pokery

The temptation will be to tell potential acquirers that you have a buyer at the table, and they need to act now. This may be a stretch of the truth, or a complete fabrication. Either way, it's an ineffectual tactic to be avoided.

The problem with this approach is that it's closed ended.

There's only so much time that any acquisition takes. More often than not, pretty soon after becoming enmeshed in acquisition discussions, a startup will go quiet with other potential suitors. As such, if after a few weeks you're still talking to PSPs to whom you've previously communicated an imminent deal, you're going to start to exude a fish-like smell.

Also, as soon as you tell a PSP that you're about to be acquired by someone else, they think they have to act under an extremely aggressive timeframe. The time pressure alone may be enough for them to back away. And, when the other deal doesn't appear to close—well, you get the idea.

You have a good chance of being exposed as disingenuous at exactly the moment you need to be thought of otherwise. There's a way to spark urgency without resorting to jiggery-pokery.

Use the process, Luke

Put a date out there.

Similar to sending out a request for proposal for a commercial project, create a letter asking for indications of interest for an acquisition of your startup. State a specific date by which you want acquisition proposals to be submitted. Make the target date for the receipt of indications three or four weeks out (not so soon it scares folks away, not so distant that it fails to generate some level of urgency). Tell the market that your board and you have decided that the highest and best use of your innovation will most likely be achieved in combination with a larger commercial entity. And that you are interested in receiving high-level indications of interest by the specified date.

The process, not a fictional suitor, is the stick.

That should be enough motivation for interested parties to act. Plus, the benefit of a process-based approach is that it's much easier to move the goalposts.

First, rather than communicating that you're imminently being acquired, all you've said is, "We'd like indications of interest by this date." A general indication of interest is a much lower hurdle for the buyer than having to immediately spin up an entire deal team, but still gets them moving in the right direction. You are less likely to scare them away with this approach.

Second, with a process-based approach, you can always move dates around. If a deal isn't completed, you own the narrative in the market. When asked about your status, you can simply say, "We are still evaluating a number of potential paths."

Urgency based on process should be compelling enough for any legitimately interested buyer. Plus, it's much more flexible for you, and the downside to not getting a deal done is much lower. If you tell a target buyer you've received a term sheet (which is also commonly called a "Letter of Intent" or "LOI") from some mysterious company, there's no substantive proof of such an offer. Hence, it will typically be received with questionable validity, or worse, as an outright bluff. In contrast, if you send the target buyer an official-looking request for an indication of interest, it feels more legitimate, and it's likely to be taken more seriously.

An official look with a better chance of getting them activated. That's a twofer.

The twist: The threat of the process

Let's add one more maneuver to our strategy of process-driven urgency. If you have a few potential targets who you think could activate quickly, you could try to get one of them to move preemptively.

First, set everything up for the full process. Don't approach this casually. You're going to need all the supporting material anyway. It's important that you look ready to go, or the urgency will drift away.

Second, call the PSP and tell them that you plan to enter a period-certain process in the near future, but that you want to give them the first look at the opportunity. They have a chance to preempt the process by making an offer now.

The beauty of this is that you've bought yourself even more time with this PSP. Not only do you have the full process still to execute, but you've added this preprocess phase as well.

You've simultaneously created urgency at the PSP while also giving them ample time to evaluate the acquisition. All of this without exaggeration or premature acceleration.

The lockup

The challenge with a process-driven approach is that the buyers will assume that the situation is competitive and will push to lock you up in an exclusive period once they've submitted their proposal.

You can add postsubmission-of-proposals steps to the process, which can enable interested buyers to begin due diligence in advance of any exclusive period (buying you a bit more time). However, you should anticipate that you'll likely have pressure from interested buyers to commit to them. Work to advance them as far in the process as you can prior to entering any form of exclusive period.

There's no perfect approach to rapidly activating buyers. I've found, however, that process-driven urgency (even with the drawbacks) typically yields the best results.

Say you get one on the line, what next?

Chapter 8

What are these guys really after?

When a PSP asks this, it means, one way or another, the startup has done everything right, at least so far. You've sent just enough signal about your openness to a deeper relationship without making your intentions completely obvious. There's been some conversation at the PSP, and now they're feeling out if an acquisition might be possible.

Here's what's going to happen next.

What is the team looking to do?

Even before price and terms, for almost every startup acquisition I've seen, the first questions from a prospective buyer are about the desires and motivations of the startup's team.

Are they mostly focused on raising capital?

Would they be interested in being acquired?

If so, are they just looking to sell this thing and bail out in order to start something else?

If they are interested in joining forces, are they really committed to the current direction because our vision is close to what they're doing but isn't quite the same?

As we discussed in chapter 4, enthusiasm matters, so these aren't just questions to be glossed over with tailored answers. These are the critical questions you need to answer. Since many, or even all, of your team members aren't likely yet in this loop, you're going to have to make some assessments on their behalf as well.

Is the buyer's organization a place you and your team can grow? Is there a strong cultural fit? Do you feel now is the right time to join forces? There's probably another book to be written on the calculus of how to answer these seemingly simple questions. For now, at least internalize that your answers are important. Hence, they should not only be pragmatic, but heartfelt.

Now, let's say the answer is that you'd like to consider joining forces, what's next?

Pace yourself

We've finally arrived at the moment at which we began in the prologue of this book. Recall, Alpha compelled an auction process and got locked into a term sheet with a long exclusive period.

Resist the urge to jump into aggressive deal-making mode. You know very little about the depth of the buyer's interest. If you go into deal-making overdrive straightaway, you'll likely set in motion a sequence of events that will result in either a bad deal or no deal at all.

Don't fall into a Popsicle-selling mindset.

Most of the injuries in Alpha's case were self-inflicted. BigCo wouldn't have locked Alpha up in a constrictive exclusive period until much later in the process, or even at all, if they weren't forced to do so by Alpha's high-pressure tactics. Then, by avoiding the resulting accelerated timetable, Alpha would have had ample opportunity to further understand, and hopefully help develop, BigCo's acquisition thesis (or realize that it just wasn't going to work). Additionally, in the more flexible nonexclusive context, Alpha would have had a significantly greater amount of time to cultivate alternative options.

Bottom line: Don't immediately rush to get a term sheet since they almost always come with an exclusive period which is not binding to the buyer but is binding to you.

Because many people continue to believe term sheets signify buyer commitment, you will likely get pressure from various stakeholders on your side of the table to ask for one. Hand a copy of this book to anyone prematurely pushing for a term sheet.

Once you have all the terms sorted out, you've tested the market to determine that the deal at hand is the right one and you're supremely confident the deal will close, then a very clear term sheet with a very short exclusive period could represent limited risk. We'll talk a bit more about how to tailor the exclusivity provisions in term sheets later.

Fortunately, once you're at that point, you probably won't even need one. I've advised on many transactions that never actually made use of a formal term sheet. We went straight from the framing of the deal to the definitive agreements.

Keep your cool

As you get deeper into negotiating an acquisition, it's very easy to get stressed out.

The acquisition of your startup is a huge deal to you. It's possibly going to change your life's future trajectory. While the deal hunt is on, it will consume you. The urgency and priority you will place on it will be like nothing else in your professional (and possibly personal) experience.

This isn't the same for the buyer. It's intriguing to them. It could even be important. But there's an imbalance in the emotional valences of the deal between the two parties. Their life isn't going to be changed by this deal. It means considerably more to you than it does to them.

This imbalance can lead to visible, and most often unproductive, frustration on your end with the buyer's pace and sense of urgency. It can be hard at times, but keeping your cool can not only get you a better deal, it can potentially save the deal entirely.

Develop a sense of the buyer's timelines, approvals and constraints. You'll find this developing understanding will not only help you identify where you are in their process but may also prod the deal sponsor in the buyer's organization to clarify next steps on their end.

Find things to do that help you relax.

Express openness to a combination

The beauty of the right approach is that it's pretty darn obvious. The first step is simply to let the other side know that you are also intrigued by the possibility of joining forces. You can say you believe your team will be enthusiastic, but at this point you're not quite ready to include them in the conversation.

Generally, it's best to not include a large group from your team in these early discussions. Avoid the temptation to discuss acquisitions internally, as you want to prevent the rumor mill from cranking up. Worse, there can be legal issues around confidentiality and even insider trading risks. Loose lips kill deals. Best to slowly expand the circle of those "in the know."

Develop the thesis

Go and meet with the buyer. Meet their team. Walk their halls and in their shoes. Meet the executives. Normally, the buyer wants to come to you and get a feel for your organization. Typically, these on-site meetings with the buyer can be positioned internally as a commercial partnership discussion so as not to raise too much awareness of the potential combination. If you feel there is a great deal of risk with an on-site visit of the buyer to your office, then it's often fine to punt the on-site visits to later in the process.

The travel that can't wait is your visit to them. Going to them will give you an enormous amount of insight into the breadth and depth of their acquisition thesis. If you arrive and the CEO takes you to dinner on the first evening, you're probably pretty well positioned already.

However, if after a couple trips to their organization you haven't met anyone above a lieutenant, your deal probably doesn't have the executive sponsorship you need.

Work with your sponsor within the buyer's organization to develop a clear understanding of what you will do together, the direction you will jointly head, an outline of product integrations, combined unit economics, rollout and so on. Have reasons and questions that require exposure to their senior executives. Don't ignore, or worse, sidestep them. You won't get to the summit without them. No one rubber stamps acquisitions.

You need to check three organizational boxes at the buyer:

Product development sponsorship: Do you have a product champion at the buyer (typically your primary sponsor in startup acquisition scenarios) who believes acquiring your startup will represent a significant advance in their portfolio of offerings?

Corporate development engagement: Corporate development and legal are the architects and engineers of acquisitions, but they aren't usually the final customer. They can't make a deal happen, though at times they can make it not happen. The challenge is they are often a shared resource across the organization, and your deal can stall if they are pulled into something with greater priority. Do you have tangible engagement from the folks you will need to process the deal?

Executive visioning: Startup acquisitions are always complex and risky. Key to the transaction's success, therefore, will be the presence on the buyer's side of one or more senior executives who thoroughly understand how the acquisition is going to be transformational for their organization. Without that solid understanding at the senior executive level, there's a good chance the deal will never make it to a close. Do you have that kind of senior executive participation?

If you can't check off all three of these boxes, you probably don't have the makings of a deal, at least not yet. It may feel like you have a deal, but in all likelihood it will fall apart before close. It takes your product sponsor, the corporate development/legal team and the executive in charge to all simultaneously turn their keys in order to successfully launch the acquisition rocket!

Start them working on due diligence

The driving thirst for early buyer commitment compels most startups to push for a term sheet before opening up their data room and initiating the buyer's due diligence. Since term sheet-level commitment is a mirage, reverse the order of the steps. Start their due diligence early.

Naturally, if there are key elements of your intellectual property, or operations, or strategy that you're not ready to share, that's fine. Let the buyer know you are holding certain sensitive folders in the data room back. The bulk of the information a buyer reviews in due diligence isn't particularly sensitive. Put a good NDA in place, one with a strong non-solicit provision whereby they can't recruit your employees or steal your customers, and let them have at it. Corporate formation, stock option plans, your office lease—who cares? Get them 90 percent through due diligence as fast as you can. Give them a clear sense that your company is nice-and-clean, and acquiring it represents very little risk.

Typically, buyers will be pleasantly surprised by your openness and happy to take a deeper look into the startup. If they aren't ready to deeply engage, then you already have your first red flag about their real level of interest in the acquisition. If they do dive in, then you will have them taking steps they would have had to take later in any case, and there are many benefits to getting those steps out of the way early. In addition, since most data room services will provide activity reports, you can begin to get a sense for both the buyer's level of engagement, and areas of particular interest or concern.

Hammer out terms over e-mail

In parallel, start an e-mail thread to discuss the parameters of the deal. Make the thread comprehensive. The benefit is that you will get more covered in this e-mail thread than you would in any term sheet. The lengthening e-mail thread will be informed by the buyer's emerging acquisition thesis.

This more fluid approach to setting deal terms yields a second benefit as well—you can now display your startup's clean slate because due diligence is already well underway. This showcase of how few risks the buyer will actually assume through this acquisition leads to a much more informed position on their part. Many of the terms you will reach with the benefit of buyer due diligence will likely be significantly more favorable than the terms the buyer would have initially proposed based on limited visibility into your startup's situation. Greater and earlier due diligence gets you better deal terms and lowers your risk!

The risk of not following the Magic Box Paradigm is that the buyer is forced to define the deal terms prior to the development of their understanding of your company, resulting in limited knowledge with which to work. They are flying blind. This lack of visibility often means starting positions on terms will be heavily skewed in the buyer's favor. The buyer wants to ensure they have the ability to protect themselves later against unanticipated obligations, such as yet-to-be disclosed litigation, or off-balance sheet liabilities. As such, in the rush to produce a "blind" term sheet, they have to set terms that are favorable to them.

By following the MBP, you create visibility and as such receive terms reflective of your actual situation, rather than terms that are protective of a worst-case scenario.

We'll dive in on the specifics of deal terms in the next chapter. The key point here is that deal terms don't have to live only in term sheets; they can live just as easily in a thread of clarifying, substantive and informed e-mails.

Time to spin up other conversations

Guess what? All of this can take weeks, or even months.

That's a good thing, as you may want time to spin up conversations with other potential targets—the ones that have shown an appreciation for your magic box's potential. Tempting as it may be, refrain from forcing their hands into any sort of rapid decision-making situation because you're having ongoing discussions with the original potential buyer. Play it a little cooler with them. Broach the topic of joining forces in general terms, and assess the levels of interest you're getting from the most likely candidates.

For example, if you learn a potential secondary target is in the middle of another acquisition or a corporate reorganization, then a hard push from you will most likely be dead on arrival. In other instances, however, even just a tiny nudge might induce a target into the acquisition discussion. Best to do some reconnaissance before dropping urgent requests for participation in your emerging process.

In particular, if the original deal falls apart, you don't want to have to answer uncomfortable questions. You can hint that you're generally thinking about joining forces with a larger player, but each conversation should be kept distinct from the other. Don't try to play potential buyers against one another. Doing so may force one of them to demand that you go exclusive with them. And that's the primary constraint you're trying to avoid. You want to keep your options open as long as humanly possible.

There are lots of ways to assess the marketplace for the possibilities of a better deal without also tipping off your current buyer that you're exploring other prospects. No need to spook the current buyer into a more aggressive deal posture.

You are usually the casualty in a bidding war

Your old school advisors will tell you: (1) get a term sheet, and (2) shop it around. But these two alleged imperatives are actually contradictory in practice—once you get the term sheet, you have no time to shop it around.

The actual imperatives for you should be either: (1) don't get into a term-sheet-requiring situation and, yes, shop around, or (2) agree to a term sheet, and don't shop around. Just don't do both a term sheet and an aggressive shopping-around maneuver at the same time. Conventional wisdom is off the mark in this case.

In a bidding war, you may succeed in driving the headline price up, but the deal will still have weeks and maybe even months before closing. That's ample time for it to fall apart (remember Alpha's fate). Better to get multiple potential buyers deep into the deal process in parallel, and then close with the one you feel is the best fit.

The potential gain of "playing buyers off each other" isn't worth the loss of optionality and the significant time pressure it puts on you. Instead, have the confidence to develop each potential acquisition thesis separately. Then, if you happen to push one or another too far or too fast, you'll have your fallback already well developed.

You may eventually end up at something close to a term sheet. But it's going to be after, and not before, the deal is well baked.

Now, let's make a deal!

Chapter 9

Coming to terms

I've seen the sorting out of the terms of an acquisition take minutes, and I've seen it take years. Just because you don't zero in on the right structure on the first pass, don't get frustrated. It just may not be the right time yet. Quite often the first conversation around terms becomes the opening of a much longer discussion. Coming to terms can require many rounds, quiet periods and also some really intense periods before the deal terms are finally nailed down. This section isn't designed to be a legal textbook. Instead, I want to give you the general coordinates for a successful business-level negotiation.

Good rule to remember: Bring in your attorneys before you start negotiating terms. Your optimal transaction structure is going to be specific to your startup. Your attorneys don't necessarily have to be on the front lines of the discussions. But their involvement ensures you're not agreeing to anything they haven't vetted.

Deal terms primer

Acquisitions are about a lot more than just headline price. In fact, depending on structure, a transaction with a lower price but elegant design may result in a better overall deal for the seller. Price is just one piece of the puzzle.

Let's break down deal terms into three primary areas of consideration:

- Economics and form of consideration
- Structure and taxes
- Risk allocation

For each of these, we are going to again break them down into their component parts. This chapter is longer than the others. For several of the major topics, I not only attempt to explain the issue as it will be presented to you, but hopefully explain how I see some of the underlying business dynamics working, thereby positioning you to negotiate from a firm footing. For some of the more peripheral topics, this chapter drops a few signposts in an effort to give you some basis for understanding them should they come up in your negotiation.

All these topics are in one chapter because when you are negotiating an acquisition they are all intertwined.

You pull on one part of the deal, and all the other parts feel the tug. The key to getting the best deal is being able to consider the interplay of all the competing forces, and then blend them together in a way that works for both buyer and seller.

Let's start at the top, with everyone's favorite topic: The price.

Economics and form of consideration

The "price" of a startup acquisition is woven from three threads:

- Ascribed value (aggregate price)
- Contingencies (things required to happen before you get paid)
- Form of consideration (cash, stock, debt)

Ascribed value

Inevitably, the buyer and seller are going to have to arrive at some broad framing of the overall "value" of the deal. In certain cases, ascribed value can get a bit fuzzy, such as when you're merging two similar businesses on a more or less proportional basis. But that's a longer topic for another book. Let's stay focused on what typically happens in most deals, where one company buys the other, for something.

As we discussed in chapter 4 (on maximizing value), the ultimate driver of price is the value of your innovation to this buyer, specifically. I hope you've followed all the steps in this book and by now have a good sense of how your current buyer wants to leverage your startup. That understanding is key to gauging the commensurate economic scale of the buyer's acquisition thesis and then in turn the amount they may be willing to pay.

Rather than rehash the buy side and sell side price drivers here, let's refer back to chapter 4 and move on to a few supporting topics around settling upon and defending the ascribed value for the deal.

We're going to break down the process of settling on headline price into three buckets:

- Who speaks first
- Defending the price
- Adjustments to the purchase price

Who speaks first

In business school, I learned a simple and useful negotiating principle: If the value of an asset is relatively determinable, then it's best for the seller to speak first and set the price negotiation starting point (in "negotiation speak" this is called setting a high "anchor"). Conversely, if the value of an asset is hard to determine, then the seller is better advised to let the buyer make the first offer, because if you speak first, you may set the anchor well below what the buyer might have been willing to pay.

Most startup acquisition negotiations fall in the latter category. It's hard to determine what the startup is worth to the buyer, so it's generally better to let the other side suggest a price first.

But the MBP has a gift for us here!

The methodical cadence of the startup acquisition process done well is going to pay a dividend to the seller. When price doesn't have to be set immediately—as might have been the case if you were racing toward completing a term sheet—your discussions can center around an exploration of the potential value to the buyer of the combination of the two enterprises. By developing that conversational direction, you're free to elaborate on any number of frameworks for assessing potential economic benefit to the buyer. You will also want to highlight, in the process, which facets of those potential benefits will derive from your startup.

This conversational direction should allow you plenty of opportunity to drop any number of subtle anchors suggesting a higher price. You want this conversation to be a foundation for the proposed price when the buyer finally comes forward with an acquisition proposal. One way or another, this conversation will have established a valuation narrative that can be useful in your eventual counter-offers or counter-arguments.

Summing up: More often than not, let the buyer initiate the pricing discussion. But take full advantage of the opportunity to provide the inputs to their calculation.

The focal point of those inputs should be utility and scarcity. As we've already discussed, the utility of your startup to a buyer (specifically what they can gain from it as part of their portfolio of offerings) drives your value to them. In turn, the part of that value they are going to be willing to share with you (as measured by the purchase price) is based on their sense of your startup's scarcity.

Defending the price

It's easy to misunderstand the place of market comparables in pricing startup acquisitions. The startup team's faulty logic goes something like this:

> *This comparable was really similar to us; in fact, they were less far along in product development than we are; and they managed to achieve such-*

and-such hefty price. Hence, we should be worth two times such-and-such price!

But this argument never works for setting price. The reasons? Comparables inevitably involve a different magic box—a magic box in different hands and a magic box on a different route to some other mountaintop.

Where market comparables can offer help is in being a more general defense of a proposed price. Rather than being a spear you use to hunt a price, they are better when shaped into a shield to defend one that's already been pinned.

Once the valuation of your startup is agreed by both buyer and seller, the immediate question from the finance people on the buyer's side will be, "How do we know this is the right price?" It's a reasonable question. You'll need a compelling answer, and ideally one that supports your price from multiple angles. Comparables can play a useful role here.

A multiple of revenue is a common valuation parameter. If revenue is growing rapidly, you can argue that the multiple should be applied to forward-looking revenue, as opposed to historical. Take care though—remember that the application of all of these concepts is negotiable and largely subjective—how you apply them will send a signal to the other side.

Startups are almost never hugely profitable at the point they're being acquired. Money has been poured into building product and scaling up the business. Hence, bottom line multiples typically look odd, so best not to bring them into play.

Startups with large or highly-valued customer bases may create a price multiple geared to the value of that asset to the buyer or the buyer's potential cost in acquiring those customers on its own. For example, if it costs your buyer $1,000 to acquire a customer, and you can deliver a million of them, then you may have a justification for a billion-dollar valuation.

Price multiples based on a startup's capital investment can justify meaningful valuations. The rationale is that invested capital represents part of the cost of the body of work to date, and that there should be a return for those who bore the risk of creating this new innovation. If millions have been invested in your startup and you can find examples of relevant comparable transactions with attractive multiples on invested capital, then such an analysis may help defend a large valuation.

When developing market comparables, it's important to look across multiple dimensions. Examine the sectors in which you operate. Look at companies acquired by buyers similar to your buyer. Examples of acquisitions by buyers similar to yours will make your buyer feel more at home in your analysis. Also look for examples of companies with similar business models, regardless of sector. Businesses based on subscriptions, or servicing enterprises, or building devices, for instance, can find great comparables in seemingly remote sectors. What will matter is that they share some aspect of important business model DNA with your startup. That shared characteristic is what makes them economically relevant to your valuation conversation.

The ideas above are just a handful of possible approaches. Be creative. Just avoid being crazy. Don't include only the highest-price comparables in your comp sheet. Offer a reasonable array. Avoid comparables operating at a completely different scale of enterprise—a company with $10 billion in annual revenue just isn't going to look relevant to one with $10 million or $1 million—no matter what other characteristics may unite them.

If you get the pushback argument that many public companies in your sector are currently trading at low multiples, the answer is often that those companies have already absorbed the relatively easy gains to be made in the market. Your startup is the new-new-thing, and as such your potential for rapid gains are greater, thereby justifying a higher multiple.

On rare occasions, it may be useful to include in your comparables analysis the valuations of companies that have recently raised venture capital funding. This sort of exercise can be problematic though. Headline valuations don't always tell the entire story of a financing transaction. Underlying dynamics (not seen in valuation), like liquidation preferences can have meaningful economic implications. These "invisible" aspects of financings can result in cosmetically higher valuations, because the terms of the investment also provide downside protections. Additionally, the amount of money changing hands is smaller, so investment-to-acquisition comparables are not only apples-to-oranges, they are small apples to big oranges.

Moreover, venture capital investors are usually quite comfortable with magic-box math and therefore tend to be less sensitive to valuation than PSPs. Their portfolio is well stocked with magic boxes. Hence, their valuations may skew high—since their portfolio's expected return is based on a stable of them—and building such a portfolio requires them to pay up a bit to get in on the best deals.

Because of all of this, investment-related comparables are a different enough animal that it's generally best to avoid using them unless they have something very clear to add to the conversation.

Lastly, it's OK to make whatever estimates and use whatever assumptions you think appropriate, provided you can adequately explain and justify your thinking. So show your work. Remember, what you're trying to build is a zone of comfort for your buyer around your deal's price and economic justification.

Adjustments to the purchase price

In more than a few cases, an agreed-upon purchase price won't actually end up being the price that's ultimately paid. Various factors will alter an agreed price along its route to becoming final. The adjustments typically derive from seller cash and cash flow dynamics.

For instance, suppose on your current balance sheet there's $10 million in cash a VC invested in your startup some time ago. If your startup is being acquired for $100 million, should the buyer get that $10 million? Now you're looking at, in effect, a $90 million deal. The answer is "no." The buyer shouldn't get that extra $10 million. That's your money, it just happens to still be in the company.

However, the mechanics of distributing cash-on-hand to your existing shareholders preclose can be complicated. The usual solution is to adjust the purchase price up that same $10 million. The newly-adjusted price becomes $110 million. It's great when purchase price adjustments are this easy. But they rarely will be.

Suppose that, instead of capital on hand, your startup has issued a very big, but as yet unpaid, invoice to one of its customers for work already performed. That's in effect your money, but where is it? If your customer had already paid the bill, those funds would be reflected in your startup's current bank balance (and folded into the previous example). But the customer hasn't paid yet. Now, your buyer and you must craft a provision in the deal reflecting a postclose adjustment to purchase price that, in effect, credits you with that late-paying customer's payment.

This process will look at both the startup's receivables and payables to determine the net working capital ("NWC") required for the seamless operation of the business. If there's a surplus above the NWC, then there can be an upward purchase price adjustment. If there's a deficiency, and you owe more than you plan to receive, then there can be a downward purchase price adjustment. Remember, such provisions can increase or decrease the deal's price. Be warned, calculations can become quite complex and quite contentious for startups with sophisticated business models.

Buyers and sellers may take quite different views on the capital required to run the business, future obligations, and many other cash flow dynamics. This disparity in viewpoints can lead to a great deal of negotiation around the formula for calculating NWC, and as a result, of purchase price adjustments. Buyers sometimes even argue that the purchase price adjustment should be able to lower the price but not increase it! To be safe, you'll want to clarify your understanding of how purchase price adjustments will be calculated when you agree on price.

Contingencies

Now we are going to move back up one level to the second major thread in determining price: contingencies.

When "closed" doesn't mean "done"

You've established a framework for how the deal is going to be valued. But there are still aspects of the deal that will stretch beyond the closing date. For example, maybe it's important to the buyer that they retain key members of the startup's team postclose. In some cases, the buyer (more often than the seller) may want to structure some kind of earnout that makes some part of the deal contingent on future performance. For the buyer, the earnout is a way of mitigating the risks associated with the acquisition. For the seller, the earnout might be a way of capturing greater upside reward.

We're going to break our discussion of contingencies into three parts:

- Earnouts aren't always great for buyers
- Earnouts can be troublesome for sellers too
- Team retention and transition

Earnouts aren't always great for buyers

Most startup acquisitions are directional. The startup that's being acquired supplies just one element in a larger strategy the buyer has developed. The buyer is acquiring a valuable technological platform and dynamic and innovative team. Both are going to greatly brighten the buyer's prospects. It is safe to say, however, that more than a few elements of the buyer's overall strategy have yet to be completely defined. This will require both teams to work in a propitious environment in which they can creatively collaborate to overcome challenges and effectively achieve the buyer's objectives.

The need for this flexible operating environment can be lost on the buyer's finance people. The finance team will sometimes look for ways to reduce the economic risk of the deal. After all, what if the buyer's long-term strategy doesn't unfold as planned? What if the startup's platform doesn't represent as much of a competitive advantage as the buyer's product team hopes it will? Doesn't it make more sense to convert a large portion of the purchase price to payments contingent on future performance? Probably not.

The first problem is that once payouts—contingent on future performance—have been installed into a deal, there's a substantial risk of killing the genie in the bottle.

Think about it. What the buyer wanted was a flexible and innovative team brought over from the startup—a team that was going to work collaboratively within the buyer's organization toward the latter's larger goals. However, once the contingent future payouts enter the picture, the startup team's focus and energies will inevitably shift toward achieving earnout targets above all else.

For example, the acquirer of the startup realizes postclose that they need a feature added to the acquired platform in order to better integrate with their existing products. However, the startup team sees the addition of this feature as a distraction from the critical-path priorities for achieving their near-term earnout target. A dispute over priorities and who is the boss of whom ensues.

This example is just the tip of the iceberg when it comes to earnouts. There's a very good chance an us-and-them mentality is now going to take shape in the combined teams. The startup has specific earnout targets to hit. Conflicts over resource allocation and operational priorities are exceedingly likely to erupt. The acquired startup team may have a sizeable reward to look forward to if future payout goals are met; the buyer side team, on the other hand, will still be working for a paycheck. These sorts of fissures can be culture killers.

Earnout provisions can also create a great deal of management and accounting complexity for the buyer. Figuring out whether an earnout target was met or not met, after all, may prove to be no simple matter. The allocation of resources, alternative accounting decisions and the navigation of any number of other organizational and economic matters can create an operational quagmire. Decisions and calculations may become topics for dispute and even future lawsuits.

The bottom line is that earnout provisions in deals can destroy more value than they create.

Earnouts work best in situations where the newly acquired startup continues to operate, postclose, as an entirely independent unit of the buyer's company. In those cases, targets can be set and measured on a truly independent basis. Conversely, once organizations are blended, earnouts become at best exceedingly complicated and at worst toxic.

Earnouts can be troublesome for sellers too

An earnout isn't always a terrible idea for the seller. The seller may have a number of considerations at play in earnout provisions. Maybe the addition of an earnout offers the only way the seller is going to achieve a desired sales price. Or maybe the seller is more or less happy with the price on the table, but an earnout offers the prospect of some additional gravy.

Even in the best of circumstances, however, earnout provisions burden deals with additional complexity. Moreover, earnouts always stretch a deal beyond the close. Costly buyer-seller differences may arise, which can even retroactively tear at the fabric of the parts of the deal that had already been thought to have been sewn up. So ask yourself, "Is the earnout's extra potential benefit really worth the potential bother?"

If you decide—even despite all the warnings I've offered—to go with an earnout, then make it as clear-cut and simple as possible. The earnout target or targets (the fewer the better) don't necessarily have to be measured in future financial performance. They can be units sold, new customers acquired or some other operational indicator. Shoot for measures you have more control over or even outcomes that are highly probable regardless what you do. Don't get mired down postclose in uncertain outcomes over which you have little or no control. Move pieces you know.

If your earnout ends up using financial measures, employ measures as far up the income statement as possible. If you can get above revenue to bookings (bookings typically being the value of customer commitments in a period, which is a higher level measure than revenue recognized in a period), it's probably a good move to even go above the top accounting line of the income statement. The further up you go, the fewer moving parts you'll need to contend with. It's harder for unforeseen events or the buyer's actions to impact a revenue number than a profit number.

One argument you can use for pushing up the financial stack is that your company is being acquired as part of an acquisition thesis based on emerging demand (as seen through topline measures like bookings, revenue, etc.). But you don't have ultimate control of the operation supporting supply (seen through bottom line measures like profit).

Earnouts can seem seductively simple at first. But, as you dig down, you'll start to appreciate the complexities they can harbor. Who controls product decisions? Who sets the budget? What if key people leave or are redeployed? What if the buyer's priorities change for completely unrelated reasons? The list of potential uncertainties goes on and on. It is simply impossible to capture every possible scenario in the earnout provision's language. Even the most meticulously investigated and articulated 100-page earnout provision would still omit any number of areas for potential future rubs.

Include clear examples of anticipated scenarios in the language. Examples will afford you some basis for shared understandings down the road.

Summing up, then, yes, there are cases where employing an earnout can be a useful strategy. However, they're the exception rather than the rule for startup acquisitions. Earnouts add complexity to deals in the short run and leave the door open for costly disputes downstream. As much as possible, move the deal to a structure that is simple, well aligned, and rests as much control as possible in your hands. Open-and-shut is almost always better than open longer.

Take stock of the situation

If the buyer is pushing for an earnout to be a large part of the deal, consider structuring the transaction in such a way that you receive equity at close, instead of a cash earnout in the future. At least equity is in your hands and not dependent on future calculations. Moreover, equity puts both seller and buyer on the same footing with respect to overall strategy. As such, it should accomplish much of what the buyer is attempting to achieve in terms of aligning incentives and motivating behaviors.

However, equity as a form of consideration can add tax-related complexity to the deal (we'll dig in on this a bit more in the later section on tax). Keep in mind, too, that equity means you'll have to stay on the economic bus until you can sell it. Look for an equity provision that allows you to liquidate some or all of your position in the not-too-distant future.

Equity in a privately-held company isn't necessarily illiquid forever. Indeed, methods of liquidating ownership positions in larger private companies have been greatly expanded in recent years. If you're receiving equity from a public company, you'll want to consider any restrictions the buyer might place on its sale, and if from smaller public companies, the volume of trading activity (it might take you a while to sell it when the time comes that you can).

Earnouts aren't perfect. Equity isn't perfect. As the saying goes, you're going to have to pick your poison.

Team retention and transition

For many buyers, the people are the startup's core asset. Retaining them is critical. In some cases, in fact, buyers will go above and beyond retention plans, requiring key team members to reinforce their postclose commitment by vesting some portion of their proceeds from the transaction.

Don't underestimate the importance of the team to the buyer. Recall the MBP's first principle that startup acquisitions are "entrances" rather than "exits"—most buyers see it that way also. Designing the more garden-variety, extra-transaction retention plans is part economics and part psychology. Retention plans that stretch too far into the future can work to constrict the relationship between the startup's team members and the acquiring company. The buyer should want the incentive to reward startup team members for making a genuine effort to fit into the acquiring organization. But the incentive plan shouldn't drag on so long that good people feel like captives in an inflexible situation.

Conversely, the buyer doesn't want to create a situation in which startup people who don't fit well into the buyer's organization hang around forever just because of the retention plan's incentive structure.

In most cases, about twelve- to twenty-four months is the right timespan for a retention plan. One to two years allows enough time for important things to happen—for a full integration of the startup team, for everyone to get accustomed to working together and for the startup's team members to discover if the acquiring company's culture is a good fit for them.

The reality is that about a year after the acquisition, the acquisition itself will likely be long forgotten. Either a good people-fit will have emerged, or not.

Another problem with long-range retention plans is that they can lack "pop." The first year is often critical in determining whether the buyer's and startup's teams are going to click or clash. Retention plans that stretch out too thinly into too long a future may not carry enough near-term gravity to hold the team in place for that first critical year.

Also, headhunters may circle around key startup players, following the announcement of a significant acquisition; they may be surmising that some real catches in the startup's team may be ready to jump to a new opportunity. You'll want a big-enough retention carrot in your deal to outweigh potential signing bonuses or other inducements some of the startup's significant players may be tempted with.

The first year is much more important than the second, third or fourth in discovering if the new combination is going to work. If the retention plan stretches beyond twelve months, I would recommend making the incentive payout for the first twelve disproportionately larger than subsequent periods, so as to maximize pop over this critical period.

There's an additional economic dynamic to consider—a startup team member leaves prematurely and relinquishes his or her remaining retention plan proceeds. Where does that money go? The three options are: (1) returned to the buyer; (2) allocated to the remaining team members of the acquired startup; or (3) paid to the shareholders of the startup. This is all negotiable. How you decide on these back-end dynamics can have significant implications on how you structure the retention portion of the proceeds at the start.

Lastly, the buyer may push back on your retention plan structure and recommendations, arguing that since their people don't receive these kinds of bonuses for continued employment, why should yours? It'll often be quite reasonable for you to make the case that your team has been cranking away with below-market compensation for quite a while. Compensation-wise, startups are often shoestring operations. Hence, the buyer should see the retention plan as also a way for the employee to make up for a history of underpayment that they have loyally endured preacquisition.

Sometimes retention plans can cause things to get a little tense

In startup acquisitions, retention plans can represent a substantial part of the value of the deal, and even the lion's share in some cases. That may not sound like a problem to the founder reading this section! But it can become a problem and can create fissures in your relationship with your investors and other nonoperating (or noncontinuing, if they are currently operating but not moving on with the buyer) shareholders.

Many buyers are intensely focused on the retention of key team members and will sometimes structure deals where the flow of consideration bears little resemblance to the actual ownership of the company. I've been witness to more than a few heated discussions between the team continuing with the buyer postacquisition and the startup's other shareholders about proposals for the way the value of the deal is to be allocated.

In fact, and this may come as a surprise, if you're a founder used to your investors having all the say on matters financial, there are times when the team has to cry foul to the buyer to ensure your investors get a fair shake in the deal.

Decisions around the division of proceeds can also have implications for the startup's board of directors. For example, it may be appropriate for certain board members to recuse themselves from decisions where there may be, or may be perceived to be, a conflict of interest. You'll want to work closely with your attorneys to appropriately steer the manner in which these decisions are made.

Team planning

One more note on transitioning the team: A deep and detailed discussion of each and every startup team member's postacquisition compensation is too big a topic for preclose discussions. The topic may well bog down wider negotiations. Still, there's nothing wrong with inserting language to the effect that startup employees will receive, at a minimum, base compensation equivalent to employees with similar roles in the acquiring organization.

Importantly, a buyer may wish to retain only a select subset of startup employees. That plan can create a significant economic burden for the startup. Think about the severance and related items that need to be accounted for. Such special-case expenses need to make their way into the overall negotiation of terms. Once again, best to surface this issue as early as possible.

Form of consideration

This is the last of our three pricing threads.

Cash is easy to understand. Cash is simple for sellers. Cash is wonderful, unless, of course, there's just not enough of it for the buyer to fully cover the purchase price.

The buyer may have other reasons for not wanting to cover the acquisition entirely in cash. Buyers, for instance, may want a portion of their payment in the form of equity in their company for motivational and other extratransactional purposes.

Beyond cash and equity, debt can also become part of a payment arrangement. The buyer may seek some financing for the acquisition from the seller. The buyer may also propose a deferred payment plan over some specified period, say, for example, in order to avoid disrupting his company's cash flow needs.

There are myriad ways of customizing the various forms of consideration that may play a role in a deal. Innovative ways can be crafted to fit the buyer's and the seller's special needs and objectives.

In the following two sections, I'm going to zero in on a couple of especially important areas to understand when structuring a deal's consideration, namely, buyer capitalization and hybrid models.

Buyer capitalization

Once you depart from an all-cash-at-close transaction, you're inevitably embarking on a journey of getting to know your buyer far more comprehensively than simply knowing their revenue model, gross margins, profit margins and so on. In evaluating and arranging noncash consideration, you need to understand not only how their business runs but how it was built and the resources taken to get to this point.

In noncash-at-close transactions, you're buying them as much as they're buying you. Naturally, the obvious question when it comes to seller-supplied financing is this: "Can, and will, the buyer make the payments?"

Assessing the buyer's ability to service your debt is critical. To this end, you'll want to have a thorough understanding of their balance sheet, any material obligations that may not be reflected on the balance sheet and any foreseen (or even potentially unforeseen) changes that may adversely affect their balance sheet. Developing this picture will not only give you the ability to assess their creditworthiness, but it's also part of your due diligence.

Some buyers may not be willing to give you their complete financial picture. In that case, you'll have to make assessments based on the available information. You can also include language in the deal that guarantees that there aren't major unspecified issues lurking in the shadows that might affect the buyer's future ability to pay.

Getting timely payments shouldn't be taken for granted. You'll need to be as sure as possible that the buyer will be able to make them all the way to the final installment.

Straight debt, by itself, doesn't align the buyer's and the seller's interests. It's really just a transaction-financing mechanism. Equity has more coaligning properties. As said in the discussion of earnouts, one of the strengths of equity is that it is in your hands, not theirs. In almost all cases, your possession of the proceeds from the transaction reduces the likelihood of disputes developing in the first place. For example, it's a much greater hassle for the buyer to try to claw back the equity they've already issued you than it is for them to rattle the sabre that they're going to withhold payments on their outstanding debt. You holding is better than them holding.

The buyer may well prefer equity to debt, because equity is essentially money they can print without having to consume cash, and will typically have a smaller footprint on their balance sheet. And as we discussed above, equity can also serve to align interests and motivate collaboration. This collaboration can even stretch beyond the startup's employees.

I've seen private-company buyers become interested in trading the seller's equity for theirs in order to have the seller's investors as shareholders in them, representing potentially newer and deeper pockets to support the buyer's own future financing needs. I've also seen buyers show real interest in adding new board members drawn from the seller's board of directors.

As you can see, both debt and equity require a deep understanding of the buyer's capitalization (and future plans), and how you fit in.

Other questions to ask are: How does the buyer's liquidation stack work? Who gets what in what scenarios? Do they have a huge capital overhang?

Are they asking you to take common stock at the bottom of the liquidation stack? And if so, how are they valuing the common stock? For example, it's not uncommon for a buyer to propose that you'll receive common stock using the price of their preferred stock as the denominator in the calculation to determine the number of shares you'll be issued—resulting in fewer shares to you. Or are they offering some form of preferred stock? Or are they even creating a new security for the transaction? All of the above are negotiable.

If the buyer is a public company and they are issuing securities to the sellers, there may be complexities around either registering those securities, or qualifying them for an exemption from registration. In either case, these logistics can have significant implications on deal structure.

Hybrid models

Not only are there many forms of consideration (cash, debt, equity) but forms can blend. Possible permutations abound. On a few occasions, for instance, I've seen convertible notes used as part of the consideration.

This approach harmonizes the seller's desire to not be at the bottom of the equity stack (and maintain the option to eventually receive cash) with the buyer's desire to incentivize the startup team to build a bigger business (and see significant equity appreciation).

If the acquirer's equity appreciates, the seller has the option to convert the note into equity. Both sides are pleased. If for some reason the buyer's equity doesn't increase in value, the seller can take the cash. And since the convertible note is due some years hence, the buyer has time to accumulate the cash for the eventual payment. This is just one example of the range of possibilities. The takeaway is that if there's a will to get a deal done, there'll be a way to do it.

Structure and taxes

This is the second major section of this chapter. We've covered price, and now it's time to figure out the best structure. As we drill down, keep in mind, eventually somewhere between 25–50 percent of the proceeds are going toward taxes, one way or another. The government is your biggest stakeholder!

First we'll tackle structure, then dive in on taxes. Naturally, the two topics are intertwined, but I find they're easier to understand if handled sequentially.

Structure

There are innumerable ways to structure transactions and, once again, even ways to create hybrids of the various major models. Nevertheless, you're probably going to see the following three main options in front of you:

- Stock purchase
- Merger
- Asset purchase

Stock purchase

One would think that startup acquisitions—where the company is owned by its shareholders—would most commonly take place as buyouts of the startup's outstanding stock. Yet, and ironically, stock purchases are the least likely of the three options I've listed. That's because stock buyouts can present substantial obstacles to acquisitions. All securities holders (including holders of warrants and options), for instance, have to individually agree to the transaction. Yet certain shareholders may not receive any return from the acquisition proceeds. Possibly, some won't like nor support the acquisition. Perhaps a big shareholder, at a crucial moment in the acquisition's progress, happens to be trekking across Tibet. It happens! There are more than a few reasons a share purchase may just not be practical to execute.

Merger

Mergers are often the best option for many kinds of startup acquisitions. Like stock purchases, they result in an acquisition of the company. They just take a slightly different route to get there. This is because mergers put forward a lower shareholder approval hurdle. Depending on the startup's ownership architecture, a merger-approving vote by a subset of all shareholders may be all that's necessary to approve a merger. All of your shareholders would then receive their postmerger consideration as part of the acquisition's closing.

For risk-mitigating reasons, however, quite often a buyer will want to have a greater number of shareholders approve the deal than simply the minimum required to effect the transaction. The greater the level of shareholder approval, the lesser the likelihood of future disputes.

Both options—stock purchases and mergers—in fact, offer significant benefits to the seller. In either case, it's likely that the bulk of the acquisition's proceeds are going to receive favorable tax treatment (i.e., as capital gains). Also, the startup's preacquisition commercial relationships should pass easily to the buyer without modification (barring a specific change of control clause in the contract). Finally, the startup's various liabilities and obligations will pass, lock, stock and barrel, to the buyer.

That last point—the transfer of liabilities and obligations—is what often motivates buyers to push for the third option mentioned above: An asset purchase.

Asset purchase

Concerns around the passage of liabilities and obligations can motivate buyers to push for asset purchase instead of stock purchase or merger. There can be financial benefits for buyers in an asset purchase as well (related to the way the value of the underlying assets is "stepped up" as part of the transaction), but most often the buyer's primary reason for proposing an asset purchase is their desire to be shielded from unknown liabilities and obligations.

Asset purchases are a way for the buyer to acquire a startup's assets without actually buying the company itself. This approach can allow the buyer to cherry-pick the most desired parts of the startup and eschew others. In doing this, they leave behind the startup as a company, and as such, if an unknown creditor comes calling, it's the seller's problem not the buyer's—the seller still being the owner of the company.

However, it's often the case with startups that the buyer is pretty much buying all the assets, leaving next to nothing behind. What the buyer is really attempting to accomplish isn't an a la carte selection of known assets, but rather a prix fixe avoidance of unknown liabilities.

Buyers will often justify their desire for an asset purchase by referencing their concerns about the startup's unknown qualities. If they don't buy the company as a whole, in other words, they don't acquire any extra legal and financial baggage.

It's a nice idea in theory. However, while asset purchases can often make sense for simple transactions, or divestitures of specific parts of the startup, in more cases than not, they're often not friendly to either side.

Here's the downside for the seller.

Asset purchases require both sides to consider each of the startup's assets and liabilities individually. This involves a tedious discussion of what's in and what's out. Invariably, the process is far more cumbersome than simply handing over the keys to the business. To add insult to injury, buyers will prefer to select the assets to be acquired but will urge the seller to attest that the assets they've picked are "sufficient" to operate the business. This provision essentially means that the buyer is picking which assets they want to buy, but it's the seller's problem if they get the list wrong! And of course, after the sale of the identified assets, the divestiture or wind down of the remaining assets consumes even more resources.

The buy side is also hampered with its own set of challenges, even though they often erroneously assume asset purchases are clean and easy for them. Continuing the MBP's stream of counterintuitive insights into startup acquisitions, consider this: Asset purchases often aren't better for buyers.

For the buyer, asset purchases open up a can of worms that can negatively impact the future operations of the assets they are so carefully trying to acquire.

One of the most burdensome aspects of asset purchases is sorting through all the startup's commercial relationships. When a startup is acquired (via a stock purchase or merger), virtually all the commercial relationships simply transfer along with the company to the new owner. In asset purchases, virtually all contracts need to be specifically and explicitly assigned to the new owner of the assets.

This means while the buyer and seller are negotiating the purchase agreement, in parallel, they may have to renegotiate every other agreement being transferred with the assets (both commercial and employment).

This could, for example, result in key commercial partners seizing the opportunity to change terms, such as increase prices, or cut off supply altogether!

As an example, say that a few years prior, you negotiated a great deal with TinkerTech, your pixie dust supplier (pixie dust being a key component in your magic box). The contract lasts for another ten years. TinkerTech, however, is fastidious when it comes to partners, so in their contract with you there is an "assignment" provision. If it comes to pass that your startup is acquired, the contract will seamlessly go along with the deal, as your company still exists as the counterparty (just under new ownership).

However, if your magic box and your company become separated, then all bets are off. TinkerTech has the right to change the terms of, or cancel altogether, the contract to supply pixie dust. In this case, because TinkerTech perceives your buyer to have deeper pockets than your startup, they decide to capitalize on the opportunity afforded them by the triggering of the assignment provision due to the asset purchase. TinkerTech revises the old contract to now be in line with their current pricing—a big increase. Rather than having a low-cost supply of pixie dust for the next ten years, the buyer gets a decade of dust at full price.

And it's not just TinkerTech, virtually every significant agreement related to the assets being acquired will have to be opened and assigned.

Don't be surprised to find your buyer going through these commercial relationships in parallel with your efforts. They will want to make sure that all obligations are met, even the ones they're not assuming. As such, an asset purchase will typically still require the same level of due diligence as the alternate structures.

As the seller, you also have to let all your commercial partners know the assets are being acquired, and by who, before the acquisition is closed. To add further complexity, there are some assets that may be difficult, or even impossible, to sell outside of an acquisition of the entire company. For example, privacy and other regulatory constraints can make the sale of customer information quite difficult when it's being sold via an asset purchase rather than a company acquisition.

Then there's still one final gotcha.

You can do all this extra work to structure the deal as an asset purchase, and it's possible the buyer won't realize the benefit anyway!

It may come to pass that the deal is "tested" to see if the asset purchase structure was just a way for the buyer to dodge certain obligations of the business. This test is called "a de facto merger test." It looks to see if the substance of the asset purchase was, for all intents and purposes, an acquisition of the company.

If it does, then poof! The golden asset purchase coach the buyer was trying to ride to the risk-free ball turns into the bright orange merger pumpkin they were desperately trying to avoid. In short, it's better for everyone if the structure of the acquisition reflects the actual nature of the underlying transaction.

In certain cases, tax implications of asset purchases can be relatively modest. However, in others, they can be deal killers. If the startup doesn't have significant operating losses to use to offset the proceeds from the purchase of the assets, then in all likelihood the proceeds will be subject to tax at the corporate level before they even make it to the shareholders. They're double taxed.

If the buyer hints at an asset purchase, get advice from the appropriate tax professionals before getting too far down that road. Don't forget to remind the buyer to speak to their tax counsel also, lest they also forgo tax benefits potentially realized via alternate acquisition structures.

In cases where a startup is selling a part of their business, or there are buyers for different aspects of the business, structuring a deal as an asset purchase can make a lot of sense. But when one buyer is scooping up what amounts to an entire startup with an asset purchase, it's worth a long conversation about what's really the best model for everyone.

Asset purchases have a way of exchanging an indeterminate number of unknown problems for a great many known ones. Not a good trade-off in most cases.

Asset purchases tend to be more common in smaller startup acquisitions, but it's good to understand them as they can come up in any number of situations. By way of another example of how creative structures can get, there's an emerging type of approach whereby the buyer acquires only a license to the technology created by the startup, along with the team, forgoing a full acquisition of the assets altogether! This speaks to the emphasis by some buyers on what teams can do in the future, rather than on what they've already done in the past.

Quick deviation on assignment and change of control provisions

Before we move on to taxes, it's important for you to be familiar with a nuance related to structuring your commercial contracts today, one that's specifically designed to come into play during acquisitions. There are basically two tiers of transfer dynamics in your commercial contracts: (1) assignment; and (2) change of control. In the asset purchase discussion above, we were referring to the "generic" form of assignment. In the generic form, when your company is acquired in a stock purchase or merger, all of your commercial contracts should flow seamlessly to the buyer as part of the acquisition. With the generic form, assignment typically only becomes an issue in an asset purchase.

However, some of your commercial partners will take an extra precaution as it relates to the transferability of your commercial relationship with them. They will seek something a bit stronger than a generic assignment clause. This higher-octane approach is called a "change of control" provision. If a contract has a change of control provision, then a review of the contract will be activated in any kind of acquisition-related transfer, regardless of structure (stock purchase, merger, or asset purchase).

As you are setting up your startup's commercial relationships, try to avoid change of control provisions; they can become a real pain during the acquisition process. It may seem like being acquired is far off in the future and that change-of-control language is of little consequence in the rush to get this-or-that contract closed today. But an acquisition may not be as far away as you think, and when that day comes, you want to be negotiating with the fewest number of parties possible!

As a final note on this, and regardless of the language in the contract, some buyers may take a conservative view on the requirement to gain consent from key commercial partners during an acquisition. For key contracts like credit agreements, or property leases, or technology licenses, the buyer may require you to gain consent from the counterparty as a condition of closing the acquisition. As the seller, the fewer of these consents the better.

Taxes

Acquisition tax dynamics are so complicated that the transaction attorneys almost always call in tax experts, and those tax experts often want to consult with tax specialists, who in turn are probably conferring and huddling with still others. And that's just on the seller's side of the table.

The key thing to remember is that tax complexities mirror deal complexities. Deal structures, earnouts, retention plans and so on, have their own (and sometimes intertwined) tax implications. Virtually every component of the acquisition agreement is a dance where consideration and taxation are the two partners.

As an example, consider provisions relating to the compensation of executives. A startup's management carve out (a designated share of the transaction's proceeds set aside as a bonus to executives to be paid upon its successful completion), or even the accelerated vesting of equity, can trigger issues related to "golden parachute payments" (also known by the regulatory section in which they are defined, Section 280g, or "280g"). As a rule of thumb, these 280g issues come up when a payment is going to exceed three times an executive's previous salary—that's a quick trigger when startup executives usually make low salaries, typically well below their market value.

That's just one example. And that one example, all by itself, can precipitate many additional actions as you work to structure and complete the acquisition. In this case, much like in the previous discussion of how retention plans can make things tense, the processes surrounding 280g dynamics can require you to make significant disclosures to your stakeholders about the distribution of proceeds and compensation dynamics of the acquisition.

By way of making my own full disclosure, tax is the topic in this book most remote from my expertise. If professional advisors (my role) are like architects and transaction attorneys are like engineers, then tax experts are like seismologists. I pass on my designs to the engineers, who in turn run them by the seismologists—sometimes they give a thumbs up, sometimes word comes back to move a wall or sometimes we have to redesign the entire building. The instructions are clear, even if the underlying physics is a bit of a mystery. That being said, in my experience, whenever possible the engineers and seismologists on both sides of the table prefer to just work most things out among themselves, only involving architects as a last resort.

There are three taxation topics that commonly arise in startup acquisition negotiations, and about which you'll want to have some familiarity:

- Capital gains versus ordinary income
- Form of consideration and tax
- Net operating losses

Capital gains versus ordinary income

In optimizing for tax efficiency, the strategy is to have as much of the consideration be classified as "proceeds" (gain on the sale of your ownership position) and as little as "income" (compensation for work). Your generic, all cash-at-close acquisition is a pretty simple structure taxwise. An all-cash-at-close acquisition should receive capital gains treatment, as your ownership position was traded for your share of the proceeds and you realize a gain or loss on your invested capital. But let's say a significant part of the value of the deal is structured as a retention plan. Or, let's say in a deal with an earnout, the decision is made that the team staying on to work at the acquirer (and earn the earnout) is going to receive a greater than proportional share of it. Or maybe the earnout has targets that pay out only if specific people are still employed by the acquirer for some period of time hence. Pretty quickly, the line between deal consideration (capital gains) and compensation for work (ordinary income) starts to blur. This blurriness is exacerbated by the fact that startup acquisitions are heavily people dependent. The deal's priorities on the buy side can center on retaining people and, as a result, the tax implications can lean away from capital gains and toward ordinary income.

As a side note, a little discussed but quite valuable tax benefit can be captured by the startup's shareholders. If your startup can meet the requirements of a "Qualified Small Business Stock" (and many can) and you've held your shares for more than five years, then some or even all of your gain may be free of federal tax. You might even be able to roll your position from one qualified small business into another inside of the five-year period. That's a huge potential win to explore.

Form of consideration and tax

As you start to move away from "cash" as the form of payment and "at close" as the time of payment, things start to get complicated. For example, if you receive some amount of equity as part of the deal, but equity represents only a modest portion of the total proceeds, you could be taxed immediately on the value of said equity. However, if the equity represents a significant portion of the proceeds, say, half or more, then you may be able to structure the transaction in a way that doesn't create any near-term tax obligations at all. This aspect of taxation can sometimes cause the seller to desire to increase the proportional role equity plays in a deal. Sometimes a modest increase in equity's role may significantly, and favorably, change the way the tax dynamics play out. But in order to classify a largely stock-for-stock deal as a tax-free reorganization (how these deals are often classified), there are a number of tests. A key test is ensuring that in the deal there isn't too much cash, or as it's called in these situations "boot." As in life, so it is in taxes, efficiency is only gained through constraints.

Naturally, this is just one example of the way that the form of the consideration can impact taxation. The key takeaway here is that you may find the tax team making recommendations that cause some significant changes to the way you seek to structure the proceeds from the acquisition.

As I mentioned at the start of this section, I thought it easier to understand the topics of transaction structure and taxes approaching them sequentially. However, in reality, since the two topics are intertwined, any transaction structure considered should be evaluated alongside the commensurate tax advantages or disadvantages.

Net operating losses

Many startups have raised and spent a great deal of capital. As such, they are carrying significant losses on their balance sheet. There are times these losses can be leveraged by your acquirer and have positive consequences for the overall transaction. However, startup founders often overestimate: (1) the utility of the operating losses to the buyer; and (2) the actual amount of operating losses they have available for use.

The founder of a startup may look at a big losses number at the bottom of their balance sheet and assume that some large portion of that number will be of value to a buyer. By extension, that number may be used by the seller as a chip in the deal's negotiation. For lots of reasons (too many to cover here), however, buyers may end up being able to realize only a portion of that value—sometimes a very modest portion or no portion at all.

The even bigger bummer is the actual amount of operating losses available for use.

Availability of operating losses for tax-offset purposes is often affected by ownership changes. Has the startup been recapitalized? Was there a down round of financing? Were there any significant changes in ownership? Many startups haven't followed a clean, linear progression in their ownership. Their ownership story since founding may have looked more like a rollercoaster ride.

A typical story goes as follows: A startup raises huge amounts of capital early on, when prospects look rosy. Over time, as development takes longer than expected, capital becomes harder to find. Investors willing to ride out the lean times with the startup take larger ownership positions as fairer weather investors see their positions reduced.

In this process, a business's ownership can shift substantially over time. And some of those changes may result in the diminution, or loss altogether, of the tax benefit derived from operating losses prior to the ownership changes. Potential operating-loss tax benefits from millions of dollars invested in early product development can be wiped away by subsequent shifts in ownership.

In a perfect world, 100 percent of the operating losses on your balance sheet will be utilizable by your buyer. However, you'll quite often find that as you start to mine the vein of your operating losses, the implications of their utility to the buyer and the amount you actually have available for use lead to the discovery of a great deal more granite than gold.

All of this said, there's also a bit of good news as it relates to taxes in deal negotiations. Buyers are often sympathetic to a seller's desire to be tax efficient, provided the proposed tax-related changes don't move too far away from, or conflict with, the buyer's interests in the deal. If they don't, and are largely mechanical in nature, you will often find the buyer willing to lend the seller a helping hand tax structure wise.

Risk allocation

We're at the last of our three major topic headings for this chapter. Remember them? They were: Economics and form of consideration (check!), Structure and taxes (check!) and Risk allocation (coming right up!).

Buyers have many reasons to want to share postclose risk with the seller. Why not, after all? Such sharing offers a way for buyers to help ensure the acquisition doesn't come with any unpleasant surprises. Buyers want protection from liabilities and obligations the seller may have failed to fully disclose during the acquisition process. They also want an easy way to collect on such claims from the seller, if and when they might arise.

Yet, the startup's sellers won't want to sign up for unlimited liability stretching long into the postclose future. The startup's founders want to buy a new house, a new car, put their kids through college. They don't want enduring risk hanging over their heads or the prospect of giving back house, car and college outlays because of a future indemnity claim. By the same token, a startup's venture capital investors will want to distribute their share of the sale's proceeds to their limited partners (the investors in their fund) forthwith; like the startup's founders, they don't want money clawed back on account of a deal that closed years ago. Sellers and their backers, in short, want deals at some point to be fully done.

Buyers and sellers in an acquisition agree on some level of seller liability for a transitional period following the acquisition's close. This process of deciding on that risk-sharing agreement I'm calling "risk allocation."

I've divided my discussion of "risk allocation" into three parts:

- Deep-dive example
- Risk splitting
- Additional considerations

Deep-dive example

Suppose you failed to disclose to the buyer that you owed $1 million to a creditor and that creditor saw the acquisition and came calling to collect the debt. In almost all cases, you and all the shareholders of the acquired startup are going to be on the hook to pay that $1 million, even though you just sold your company.

That example is pretty straightforward. I bet you get it.

Now let's dive deep. Let's say you built a new gizmo, let's call it Gizmo-A. You and your team have been heads-down building Gizmo-A for years—it's really cool.

BigCo acquires Gizmo-A for $100 million (this time BigCo gets the deal all the way to the finish line!).

However, in the definitive agreement to acquire Gizmo-A, BigCo inserted a clause that says that if you know, or should have known, that Gizmo-A infringes on someone else's patents, you are responsible for up to 100 percent of the purchase price ($100 million) for any damages

BigCo realizes. Time passes, and with BigCo's help, Gizmo-A becomes a huge success.

However, HugeCo, BigCo's sworn enemy and competitor, is jealous of this new product. They've been locked in a number of patent lawsuits for years with BigCo and are always looking for a reason to pick a fight. HugeCo searches their patents and finds one that kind of looks relevant to Gizmo-A. It doesn't look like an exact match, but it's close enough to kick up a fuss. Maybe they can extract some concessions from BigCo on some other front by opening up this new one. Or maybe they'll get lucky and directly win a patent infringement lawsuit against BigCo over Gizmo-A. Either way, it's always a win for HugeCo to take the fight to BigCo.

HugeCo gets lucky. It turns out the patent was close enough to describing part of how Gizmo-A works that the court awards HugeCo a $100-million judgment against BigCo for Gizmo-A's infringement on HugeCo's patent.

BigCo pulls up the Gizmo-A acquisition agreement, which says you are responsible for any infringement of which you "should have known." According to BigCo, everyone should know the ins-and-outs of HugeCo's patent portfolio! You should have known!

BigCo demands their $100 million back, and after a drawn-out legal fight between BigCo and you, you're forced to give it to them.

Is this fair?

No. Arguably, it's not fair.

There are some risks a buyer has to absorb if they decide they want to compete in a market. These market participation risks are beyond the scope of what a startup should be asked to underwrite when they are acquired.

What if rather than acquiring Gizmo-A, BigCo had independently developed Gizmo-B? It took them longer to get it commercially viable, it wasn't as cool as Gizmo-A, and it cost them $300 million to develop. But given the strength of their distribution channels, they are able to turn it into a successful line of business.

HugeCo still hates BigCo, still cooks up the same reason to sue them, and still wins, like in the previous scenario.

However, now it's BigCo that has to absorb the $100-million judgment to HugeCo as it was their decision to enter the market and they who decided to build Gizmo-B. It's 100 percent BigCo's problem. They can't pass it off to your startup.

Just as in the first scenario, they didn't know about HugeCo's patent or maybe did know but made a calculated bet that HugeCo wouldn't be able to win an infringement suit. Either way, it was a business decision on BigCo's part as to whether or not they wanted to be in the Gizmo business. They decided to enter in spite of the fact that one of the risks of being successful in a line of business is that people try to sue you, and sometimes they win.

So, if BigCo builds Gizmo-B, they have to absorb the risk, but oddly, if they acquire Gizmo-A, you have to absorb the risk. Does that seem fair? Maybe not.

BigCo, like any buyer, needs to shrewdly assess the competitive landscape and the intellectual property risks of participating in a market. It's absurd to attempt to push those risks onto a startup. In our example, why should you be expected to be on the hook for the collateral damage from the feud between HugeCo and BigCo?

Acquiring Gizmo-A represented a faster and cheaper approach to entering the Gizmo market for BigCo than building Gizmo-B on their own. Once in the market, the risks of participation should be the same for BigCo regardless if they acquired or internally developed the product. Just because they chose to buy rather than build shouldn't mean they, all of a sudden, get to have the seller underwrite the myriad risks they would have otherwise had to absorb on their own.

To be clear, if the Gizmo-A executive team had knowledge that they were infringing on the intellectual property of a third party, then they should be on the hook if that wasn't disclosed. And it's always reasonable for buyer and seller to have a conversation about where IP risks may exist in the market.

But the notion that they "should have" known is unfortunately common in acquisition agreements and leaves the door open for any number of startup-unfriendly interpretations.

The way that risk was allocated in the purchase of your startup in this example was unfair. You were caught in a battle not of your making, and killed in the firefight.

Hopefully, this example highlights how important the allocation of risk is in an acquisition agreement.

Risk splitting

The BigCo example is why we are going to base the discussion of how to decide who bears which risks on the following two positions:

- The entry or expansion of your buyer into a market is a business decision for which they are ultimately responsible (we'll call this "market participation risk")

- The seller is responsible for the bona fide nature of the startup and issues known at the time of the acquisition (we'll call this "acquisition risk")

Risks related to market participation should ultimately be risks the buyer should largely absorb, as BigCo should have in their war with HugeCo. Risks related to the bona fide nature of the startup should largely be absorbed by the seller, as in the earlier example where you forgot to mention you owed someone $1 million.

This discussion of risk-splitting is broken into three parts:

- Fraud and fundamental representations and warranties
- General representations and warranties
- Intellectual property representations and warranties

As another reminder, this is not a legal textbook. I am not going to dive deeply into the technical nuances and varying interpretations of the legal terms I discuss. Instead, I'm going to consider these concepts broadly to help you understand some of their practical implications and where they come up in the business-level negotiations. Hopefully, this discussion better enables you to make informed assessments and decisions.

Fraud and fundamental representations and warranties

In the acquisition agreement, misrepresentation of important facts is almost always made the seller's responsibility.

If you're shown to have intentionally misrepresented a material fact or intentionally concealed one, that's called fraud, and you're going to be on the hook for the consequences. And fraud isn't to be taken lightly as, unlike most other liabilities, there's often no cap on your exposure for fraud-related claims. The more you document and disclose, the less likely you'll be accused of misrepresentation or concealment.

Fundamental representations and warranties ("fundamental reps") relate to the core nature of the startup. If there's a problem in how the company itself was formed or in some other "fundamental" aspects of the business then these problems, in all likelihood, are going to be your responsibility should an issue arise postclose. The liability for fundamental reps is often capped at 100 percent of the proceeds from the acquisition.

For example, say you have a number of shareholders who, for some reason, were not captured on your list of shareholders when the proceeds from the deal were distributed. After the acquisition, they return to collect their share of the proceeds. It is your responsibility to pay these forgotten shareholders their rightful share. The buyer is not culpable for this unforeseen outlay because you failed to give them a complete list of shareholders. Having a complete list of shareholders is pretty fundamental.

Capitalization (shareholders), formation (was your company created correctly), taxes, and certain employee matters are commonly included in the fundamental reps. In addition, and depending on your company's business context, a few other areas can be pulled into the fundamental reps too. One example might be reps related to environmental matters, which can be an important factor in some acquisitions. Lastly, you'll want to discuss with your attorneys the scope and duration of your liability for fundamental reps, general reps, and even for areas not covered in the acquisition agreement at all.

General representations and warranties

General representations relate largely to the operation of the business.

Recall the example at the start of this section where you forgot to disclose you owed a creditor $1 million, and had to pay for it. Those are the sorts of liabilities that are covered under general reps. There's a little more leeway in these "general reps." This leeway derives from the reality that no business can completely document every aspect of its operations. Most acquisition agreements will include language setting out the hurdles a future claim has to clear in order for it to merit a payment from the startup's sellers. Naturally, and because of this leeway, the buyer wants to define the general reps as broadly as they can, and the seller as narrowly.

A second dynamic in play is that the buyer won't want to confront obstacles, postclose, in collecting payments that have cleared the aforementioned hurdles. To this end, the buyer and seller may agree to a fixed set-aside amount drawn from the sale's proceeds. That set-aside will cover any claims arising from breaches of reps and warranties for a predetermined time. Typically, this money is escrowed in a third-party account.

The primary business-level dynamics in settling breaches of general reps and the role of the escrow are:

- How much is covered and how much goes into the escrow?
- How long does the coverage last and how long does the escrow last?
- The role of "knowledge"

The hurdles the buyer must clear in order to make a claim will probably be largely scaled to the deal, and the buyer's and seller's attorneys are usually able to find a middle ground on the inner technical workings of the escrow. But the three areas above will often elevate to a business-level discussion, so it's important you're aware of what they mean.

To help you in finding a reasonable middle ground with the buyer, there can be found online some very useful third-party publishers of M&A deal terms data. These sources give benchmarks and trends for how representations and warranties are structured, the typical scale of escrows, the frequency of various provisions and so on.

You will find that the risk averseness of your buyer and your buyer's assessment of the range of potential issues associated with the acquisition will ultimately shape their position on the general reps.

A few more background items to cover

From a deal-making standpoint, I would strongly recommend you don't leave the discussion of reps and warranties until late in the process. Include the baseline expectations for reps and warranties into the outline that contains the deal's consideration and structure.

I can't recall a time when waiting or delaying the initiation of the reps and warranties conversation improved the seller's position. It's not a topic the buyer is going to skip over later. If you wait until late in the process to structure this part of the acquisition, you will likely receive less favorable terms because the pressure to close will be greater on you than on the buyer. You'll bend.

Instead, early on, proactively place a reasonable proposal for how to handle representations and warranties, and the escrow on the table for your buyer. Push the buyer to affirm that what you've proposed will be present in the final framework; that is, should it come to pass that nothing significant that's relevant to the reps and warranties is discovered during their due diligence process.

Even though this confirmation from the buyer may not be formally binding, there's some level of pressure to not change something already agreed upon earlier in an acquisition. If they do try to change this part of the deal later in the acquisition negotiations, having good documentation of your shared prior understanding may at least strengthen your bargaining position, say for example, by giving you an opportunity to cede concessions on reps and warranties for gains elsewhere in the negotiation.

One more practical point to make: Under normal circumstances, sellers typically lose leverage the further they get into the acquisition process. However, if you're following the MBP, then you're sharing information much earlier than you would have otherwise with your buyer and moving a significant amount of what typically happens later in an acquisition to much earlier in the process. This increases the pressure on you to be fully prepared on a wide array of the deal's potential elements, but maintains your negotiation leverage throughout the process.

If the buyer senses that your startup is a well-run operation and that your presentation of information about it is tight and well organized, then the buyer will typically be more comfortable that there aren't unknown liabilities lurking in the wings. That will tend to tilt the buyer toward a friendlier stance of reps and warranties too.

However, when your data room is a mess and every time they ask for information you stall, only to later supply them with 75 percent of what they were asking for, then they will start to sense there's a nontrivial chance you've missed some form of liability. Their risk of needing one day to lodge postclose claims just jumped up a notch.

Being well prepared and responsive during negotiations increases your chances of receiving better terms.

Now, let's dive into the three primary negotiation points we outlined above.

How much is covered and how much goes into the escrow?

First, be mindful that the set-aside amount you put into the escrow may not necessarily cover all possible postclose liabilities that surface. Your potential liability can be larger than the amount set aside and your liability may extend well beyond the end of the escrow period (we'll discuss this in the next section).

Ideally, your buyer will agree that the escrow represents the "sole and exclusive remedy" for any (and all) postclose claims. Getting them to do so may be a tough sell for fundamental reps. Yet, for most startups, defining the escrow as the sole and exclusive remedy for general reps should be achievable. Again, you need to bring this up early in the definition of the deal terms. If you don't, you might very well wake up one day to find that you've been muscled into providing the buyer with a much broader coverage package than you contemplated at first.

As it relates directly to the escrow, the percentage of the proceeds placed in it to cover claims will be agreed between you and the buyer. Naturally, the exact amount varies by deal. The key is to work with your attorneys, advisors and the third-party research to come up with a reasonable sense of the typical size of the escrow in deals broadly similar to yours. For deals on which I've advised, the size of the escrow has typically been 5–15 percent of proceeds.

How long do indemnity coverage and escrow last?

As noted already, your liability with respect to postclose claims may extend in time beyond the end of the formal escrow period. Therefore, to the greatest extent possible, seek to have the escrow defined as the sole and exclusive remedy for as many types of postclose claims as possible. Defined thus, the escrow parameters will match the caps on both the size and duration of your postclose liability.

Postclose claims against the escrow are typically going to surface in the first few months after close. By a year out, the deal is already becoming ancient history, and the likelihood of a large claim still being lodged recedes to pretty small.

Hence, my rule of thumb is that twelve months represents a workable period for the escrow's life. Some buyers will push for longer escrow periods. If you get stuck arm wrestling with your buyer over its duration or size, one possible compromise is to devise an escrow whose amount declines over time, with funds released to you at specified intervals. The logic here is that the escrow amount should reflect how risk declines with the passage of time. It's your money and it shouldn't be held hostage indefinitely.

The role of "knowledge"

In the first draft of pretty much every acquisition agreement I've seen, there are many definitive declarations to which the seller will be asked to attest. For example, that you comply with every regulation ever created in every country, and on the moon. If you agree to this declaration as it is first drafted, then you're on the hook if it can be shown later that you in fact didn't comply with some obscure regulation. What your attorneys will do is go through the agreement and soften some of the language, and equally important add what is called "knowledge qualification."

So, the declaration will be modified to say something like "to the seller's knowledge they comply with relevant regulations." The softening is important, but the knowledge qualification is even more important. By adding the knowledge qualification, you've essentially transferred the risk from the seller to the buyer, reclassifying it as market participation risk and not acquisition risk. If you didn't know about an issue that later comes up and it's in a section with a knowledge qualification, then it's probably going to be something the buyer has to absorb and not the cause of a future claim against you.

Naturally, your lawyers are going to sprinkle knowledge qualifiers throughout the agreement, while the buyer's lawyers conveniently sweep them away. There are a great many places where they are completely reasonable.

You think we'd be done there, but we're not. In an acquisition agreement, the tree of knowledge has two important roots. The first root is the definition of the term "knowledge" itself. The second is who is included in the group of people defined as possessing acquisition-relevant knowledge.

First, we'll tackle the easier of the two roots: The definition of the term "knowledge." Frequently, a buyer will attempt to define knowledge as it was defined in the

BigCo acquisition of Gizmo-A. A definition that includes both what the seller knew and should have known. You're going to want to lop off the second half of that sentence. You want the definition of knowledge to only include things the seller actually knew. Period.

As we've discussed previously, the buyer has to make their own assessment of the risks associated with this new or expanded market participation. Once the word "should" is in the definition of knowledge, there is a transfer of market participation risk from buyer to seller. No thanks.

If the acquisition agreement to acquire the Gizmo-A hadn't had the world "should" in it, then Gizmo-A's inventors would have been able to keep their $100 million.

Shoulda, woulda, coulda.

The second root is the question, "Who knows?" You want the pool of people included in the definition of knowledge to only be key executive team members. These are the people in a position to roll up information and make assessments of its importance at an organizational level.

Risks evolve over time; something that may become a commercial risk years after the acquisition could have begun its life years before the acquisition. It just didn't register on the startup executive team's radar as a potential threat at the time of the acquisition. The potential that these amorphous forces could shape into future risks is something the buyer has to absorb, and is the price they pay for participating in this market.

The reason it should only be senior executives included in the definition of knowledge is that including every person in the organization in this definition casts an unreasonably wide net for objects that may, or may not, emerge as postacquisition threats to the business.

Said differently, your kid's knowledge of a seed in the dirt in your neighbor's backyard is a far cry from your knowledge of your neighbor's tree that's about to fall on your house. The former is an object of no threat today, and may never become one. The latter object is clearly a known cause for concern. It's in everyone's best interest to focus on the trees and not clutter the conversation with the discussion of every seed.

As such, there needs to be a reasonable filtering process for what represents relevant knowledge. As a practical matter, the filter should, essentially, sort for objects of concern to senior executives at the time of the acquisition. Naturally, that's not legal language, but you get the idea. And the objects caught by that filter are ones your startup is probably going to have to absorb.

The objects the filter doesn't catch should probably be sorted into the box of market participation risks, and as such should typically be absorbed by the buyer.

Intellectual property representations and warranties

We're at the last of our three major topic headings under risk splitting: Intellectual property representations and warranties ("IP reps").

If the case of BigCo versus HugeCo didn't heighten your awareness of this issue, I don't know what will!

Since much of the risk related to intellectual property results from the use of the intellectual property by the buyer, IP risks are, for the most part, market participation risks. As such, IP reps should be, and typically are, bundled into the general reps.

However, some aggressive buyers may push for IP risks to be treated as if they were elements of the deal's fundamental reps. Doing so may put as much as 100 percent of the proceeds of the deal at risk for the seller.

The buyer's argument in such situations goes something like this:

> *Look, we're buying this company because of its technology, and we're paying a great deal of money for it. Don't you guys stand behind the originality of your platform?*

Of course, you stand behind your platform's originality. But IP is a funny critter. It doesn't have a fully definable, point-to-point character, such as a contract with a supplier that you may have inadvertently forgotten to drop into your data room. IP issues are inherently multidimensional and can emerge for all kinds of reasons. Their magnitude, moreover, may be unknown to the seller and the buyer during the acquisition process. And their meanings may be subject to widely differing interpretations.

Little-company IP problems are different from big-company IP problems. A patent troll or a larger competitor may not want to bother with trying to shake down or attack a small-market player. But targets with deep pockets or companies posing potential competitive threats may attract exactly that kind of hostile interest.

No matter what approach to the technology the buyer takes (e.g., either securing the technology by buying you, or by developing it themselves), their competitors may still see some advantage by launching an IP-based attack at some point. In which case, you definitely don't want to find yourself in the middle of a them versus them firefight.

It's understandable why the buyer would want to charge back the cost of IP challenges to the seller. But that sort of seller responsibility is something the startup should usually reject. The buyer is inevitably responsible for making their own assessment of IP-related risks they may face by incorporating the startup's technology into products they offer the market. Zero in on IP issues early in the framing of the terms. Make it clear that you see it as the buyer's job to make their own assessment of the IP risks associated with participating in this market. Confirm that IP reps are included in general reps. Articulate that you don't plan to underwrite their market participation risk.

Additional considerations

You've hammered out the price, form of consideration, structure and risk allocation! Woot!

There are just a few additional topics we need to briefly discuss before we turn to closing the deal in the next chapter.

Representations and warranties insurance

If it looks like you and the buyer are just too far apart on representations and warranties, it may make sense to look into finding insurance to help resolve the issue (yes, there is such a thing as reps and warranties insurance!).

In particular, if your startup is backed by institutional venture capital firms, you may find that your investors take a very strong position on the need for caps on liabilities. Insurance could be a great tool in such cases.

A number of providers offer this sort of coverage and the cost may be as low as a few percentage points of the amount covered. A timely use of insurance may help bridge an otherwise problematic gap between the buyer's and seller's positions on risk splitting.

Escrows over holdbacks

Particularly in smaller deals, the buyer will prefer to structure the reserve for claims as a holdback rather than setup a third-party escrow. A holdback means the buyer holds on to the money, less any claims, until an agreed future date. Whenever possible, opt for an escrow over a holdback. Escrows provide one more layer of protection for the seller against any unanticipated maneuvers by the buyer. Holdbacks, however, can turn into "holdons," in which you never get the money.

The escrow's role in purchase price adjustments

As we covered earlier in the section on purchase price adjustments, postclose economic dynamics can result in changes to the acquisition price paid by the buyer. Some of those machinations can be handled via your escrow arrangements. Make sure, therefore, that your discussion of the escrow with your attorneys includes both (a) the handling of claims for breaches of representations and warranties; and (b) the settlement of posttransaction adjustments to the purchase price.

Skullduggery, shenanigans and misunderstandings

The buyer of a startup is typically bigger than the seller. The buyer thus has greater resources and has a larger legal team. This underlying asymmetry means that resolutions to disagreements that pop up after the close will, as a practical matter, likely lean in the buyer's favor. Put another way, it'll likely be too costly and too painful for the seller to spin up an adequate legal team to fight postclose claims and issues. This is not to say that all buyer postclose claims are illegitimate. Postclose circumstances can sometimes arise in which compensation to the buyer from the seller may be appropriate and fair. These times shouldn't be confused with attempts by the buyer to exploit their size asymmetry and the "hassle imbalance" the postclose situation affords them. Once the deal is done, it's just typically the case that the buyer's negotiating position is stronger than the seller's. Hence, as a general rule, as the seller, make every effort to leave as little as possible "out there" for possible postclose buyer pushback.

Deals penned in black are better than those in gray. Proceeds in your hands are more secure than proceeds in theirs.

With that warning, the section on risk is a wrap. You've made it through!

Two more points to keep in mind during the negotiation process

Last two topics for this chapter: Term sheets with exclusivity provisions and Breakup fees.

Term sheets with exclusivity provisions

If you haven't picked up on it already, I'm not a big fan of exclusive periods.

But if you get deep into the deal and a serious buyer is insisting on a term sheet with an exclusivity provision, here are a couple maneuvers you can use to keep things moving apace.

Make sure the term sheet includes two elements:

1. A fixed date by which you receive a comprehensive draft of the definitive agreement from the buyer's lawyers: Getting the lawyers involved tends to show real commitment to the deal and requires lots of internal approvals on the buyer's end. You aren't going to get a draft definitive deal document from them if they aren't seriously interested in the acquisition. By extension, then, your request for one gives you an acid test of how serious their interest actually is. And it's better to know that sooner rather than later!

2. An explicit understanding that any buyer-initiated proposed changes to the deal's terms or any decision by the buyer to disengage from the deal must be communicated to you immediately, say within forty-eight hours of their determination. This second provision acts like truth serum. It ensures that the buyer can't dribble away your valuable time while secretly scheming to change the deal.

The triggering of either provision gives the seller the right to immediately terminate exclusivity. These protections aren't perfect, of course, and it's better to avoid going exclusive whenever you can. But these two tweaks will at least give you a modicum of leverage during the time you're barred from engaging in other conversations.

Remember, the term sheet (or LOI) is almost always the high-water mark of the terms you're going to receive in the definitive agreements. If you're lucky, they'll stay the same; if you're not, they'll get worse. The terms are almost never going to get better. As such, delay entering a term sheet for as long as you can, push the buyer to complete all the due diligence humanly possible and shorten the time between entering the exclusive period and when the deal is completed.

Breakup fees

Breakup fees are a payment to the seller if and when the buyer walks away from the deal. They're actually not a common element in startup acquisitions.

They're tough for the seller to negotiate and tend to drain momentum from the main act: the development of the terms of the acquisition. As a practical matter, they also can be difficult to collect. So they need to be very tightly structured, and the breakup fee amount, whenever possible, lodged in an escrow. Even then, however, one must be mindful that the buyer may be able to cook up some plausible looking reason for backing out without paying the breakup fee. There are almost always going to be valid looking excuses or justifications they can muster to explain why they chose to back out of the deal.

In any case, the breakup fee probably isn't going to be commensurate with the damage their backing out of the deal has done. Breakup fees are a poor substitute for a comprehensive execution of the MBP. It's better to focus on creating and maintaining multiple options during the acquisition process than try to rely on the false security of term sheets and breakup fees.

Now, let's close this thing.

Chapter 10

Closing

The mountain gets steepest at the top

You've done a masterful job up to this point. You've developed a powerful acquisition thesis around your magic box. You've hammered out comprehensive terms. You've artfully overcome the issues that once threatened to kill the deal. Now, onto the summit!

This section isn't about what the two legal teams have to do to achieve a final close. I never cease to be amazed by how much hard work attorneys put into fully closing acquisitions. It's brutal. They will have closing checklists and they'll help you understand the technical dynamics of the closing process. This section instead covers a few essential components you need to know at a business level so that you're ahead of the game when these dynamics come into play.

Full disclosure

This is topic numero uno for an important reason. You've come a long way. The end is in sight. The temptation, and even the pressure, is going to be strong now to not introduce any additional topics that could delay or derail the close. Resist this urge. Whatever that lingering topic may be, it's almost assuredly going to come out eventually. And, in the grand scheme of things, it'll only be worse the later it comes out.

Starting due diligence earlier (as part of your practice of the MBP) will by now mean that there aren't significant matters still to be hashed out with the buyer. But if there are, now's the time to put them out there and sort them out. If an item is relatively small, then the seller is foolish not to deal with it straightaway. Left to fester, the buyer might eventually construe it as having been a bigger issue than it actually was. If an item is a big issue, then the seller is crazy to not lay it out fully. If its disclosure is delayed beyond the close, it may morph into a serious problem down the road.

Your attorney or the buyer's attorney will give a very long due diligence checklist, and you will be asked to fill out an extensive set of disclosure schedules for the definitive agreements. I've heard more than one attorney characterize the disclosure schedules as a "get out of jail free card" for the seller. Postclose issues can't grow like weeds when they've been fully disclosed preclose. On the other hand, undisclosed issues have a way of cropping up postclose when you least expect them. It is in the seller's interest to fully, fully disclose.

I hope you've followed the MBP and initiated due diligence early, putting everything on the table while you were sorting out terms. If you haven't, bite the bullet now and lay it all out there.

Expanding the circle

Up till now, you've probably been able to handle most of the acquisition process with a small team—comprising just your board and a few key executives. Such things as meetings with buyers, developing their thesis, building the data room and hammering out broad terms were all things that could be handled with the help of this small group. But now, the requests are getting more specific. The buyer wants to meet more people from the team. It's getting tougher to keep the lid on things.

There's no perfect way to manage these dynamics. But, since the deal isn't closed and could still fall apart, you'll want to be pretty thoughtful about how you communicate the acquisition situation to the widening circle of participants.

First, it has to be made exceedingly clear to everyone you involve that this entire topic is highly confidential. Not only could word leaking out kill the deal, there's real risk of insider trading, as well as a number of other daunting concerns. People may lose their jobs. They can go to jail. Stress the crucial importance of confidentiality. Then stress it again.

Second, manage expectations. People get psyched up about acquisitions. They start to see themselves updating their resumes, calling their mom, buying a new car. Emotions well up. Hence, it's important for you to insert a very healthy dose of don't-count-your-chickens reality into the situation. There's still a nontrivial chance the acquisition unravels. In that event, you will want your team to view the process as an indicator that you're on the right track and that innovative companies attract acquisition interest—it just didn't click this time.

Nourish internal narratives about the meanings of both the deal happening, and not happening. Then, if a hoped-for deal ends up not closing, you won't be regarded as "spinning" the failure to your people. You, and they, will have a mindscape into which you all already fit.

Third, prepare your team for communication with the buyer. Some of your people will be natural communicators; others, not so much. If your team members are going to a meeting with the buyer, have them prepare slides in advance to which they can speak, and have them practice. A little bit of preparation will help them showcase the importance of their area of the organization and also give the buyer a better sense of your team's depth and strength.

Fourth, ensure that your board and key stakeholders are informed and involved in making the important decisions. You don't want to make a long list of agreements with the buyer and then discover your board and shareholders are never going to agree to many of them. If it's a homerun deal and all of your shareholders are "in the money," then you'll probably have a pretty easy time aligning interests. However, for all other deals (that being most of them!), work with your attorneys to help your key stakeholders understand the positions and trade-offs, and ensure everyone is keeping pace with the decisions being made. This will also enable board members and shareholders to provide input into difficult choices and align themselves with the startup's decisions. For instance, a decision you're completely comfortable with may not work for structural reasons for your venture capital investors. It's critical to surface these kinds of constraints early.

Naturally, the right processes and procedures will vary from organizations to organization. Follow the general principle that your stakeholders don't want to be surprised, and neither do you.

Definitive agreements

The definitive agreements for acquisitions are long and boring. It's easy to assume that they are full of boilerplate language that's not important to read. The language isn't just boilerplate. It's important to read and read carefully.

Some sections are common to all or nearly all acquisition agreements. Yet, and inevitably, some terms will be entirely specific to your startup and your buyer. The attorneys attempt to create language that reflects their best understandings of the buyer's and seller's intentions and the underlying characteristics of the business trading hands. But that's often not easy to do, and the attorneys won't get everything 100 percent right. You are the person who knows your business. You need to read the language and make sure it matches your intent for the deal.

Get out the highlighter. Dig in. Ask lots of questions. If the language relates to economics, build a spreadsheet, run scenarios based on the language and see if they actually calculate out the way you believe they should. Read the deal backwards. Consider examples. Ask more questions. These words are the deal. Years from now, should a dispute arise, it's not going to matter what Sue or Harry remember or think they remember about the deal. What was said over dinner before the deal closed isn't going to matter either. The deal's actual words are going to be what's pulled up and gone over with a fine-tooth comb.

Team matters

There are many dynamics at work when teams transition from one organizational structure to another. I wouldn't be the person to provide a comprehensive list, and the list would probably require another book anyway. Compensation schedules, benefits, stock options, policies and so on, all play in the change. Generally, there will be people on the deal teams to help you sort through all this stuff. The issues are not unfamiliar to experts in their fields, and they typically have pretty straightforward answers.

However, one notable transition issue that will likely find its way to you is more emotional than legal. It concerns the roles of senior startup team members in the buyer's organization. For instance, your cofounder, before the acquisition, may have had the title of Chief Technology Officer (CTO). Postacquisition, however, their responsibilities become more akin to those of a director-level engineer (managing a specific product team in an organization with a hundred product teams). The former CTO isn't terribly happy about the appearance of a demotion. There's nothing wrong with engaging in a discussion of postacquisition roles, responsibilities and job titles before the close. But it'll be best to avoid initiating broad HR reviews concurrently with your efforts to complete the acquisition.

The real story for your team's members is this: They were a valued part of the startup that got acquired, and they continue to be a valued part of the team that got retained in the acquiring company. That's the message for their resumes. Moreover, it's not the end of the world to take on fewer new responsibilities in the acquiring organization versus an inordinate number of new ones if elevated to an executive role. Starting smaller may afford time to learn the company's management style, culture and organizational dynamics. Starting at the top, on the other hand, reduces that time and creates a steeper and more visible learning curve. Lastly, larger organizations tend to be more bureaucratic than startups. Does the CTO really want to stop coding and start on the meeting circuit? Boring!

Noncompete agreements

Don't be surprised if the buyer wants language limiting the startup team's members from competing with them in the future. Attorneys will help you sort through this aspect of the agreement.

There are three big elements in competition-limiting provisions: Who signs these provisions? How is competition defined, exactly? How long do they last?

The "who signs them" question should be dependent on relative reward from the acquisition. To ask someone receiving a miniscule part of the acquisition's proceeds to take themselves off the competitive market in their industry is untenable and unfair. Noncompetition should only apply to the bigger winners in the acquisition.

Defining "competition" is a tricky one, but generally it should map to the nature of the startup being acquired, not to the nature of the company making the acquisition. The former being a closer proxy for the expertise the buyer is trying to restrict from general availability.

The "how long" question centers on when the noncompete starts. For instance, does the noncompete expire with the passage of x amount of time starting from the deal's close? Or does it expire in y amount of time starting from the moment an employee elects to leave the acquiring company? In my experience, the former is preferred. As a general rule, the more time since the acquisition's close, the less relevant the noncompete provision becomes for former members of the startup team.

The important thing to note is that noncompetes need not be one-size-fits-all. Specially crafted terms and scopes may be devised to match the context of the deal and individual.

Completing the agreements

You will have many rounds of redlines, innumerable conference calls and even a few "all hands" meetings to sort out key issues once and for all. It's all part of the process. There may also be times when the attorneys just can't come to a resolution. In those cases, it's probably best for you to get on the phone with the decision maker at the buyer (and knowing who that actually is and having their ear are also part of the job!) to discuss the troublesome issue person-to-person.

Good lawyers are masters at making you believe that their positions descend directly from stone tablets. However, what you will very often discover is that the issue on which the buyer's attorneys are stuck isn't even what the buyer is worried about in the first place. The buyer's attorneys just made you believe it was.

On the phone with the buyer, you'll be able to drill down to the root cause of the concern and find creative solutions where others found only impassable roadblocks. Don't approach these conversations as confrontations. Approach them as obstacle courses that you and the buyer are going to figure out how to navigate. Start by asking questions, not by making demands. You'll find most often that an issue unpacks on its own and together you'll be able to come up with a mutually agreeable solution.

The close

Even the act of closing isn't as simple as you may have thought or hoped! For many startup acquisitions, it should be possible (and preferable) to have a simultaneous sign and close. This means the deal documents are executed and the close happens (i.e., you get paid) at the same time. But sometimes special hurdles make that sort of simplicity impossible. Shareholder approval or regulatory considerations may intrude or the buyer's financing ducks may not be fully lined up. The challenge with signing on one occasion and closing on another is that a new set of risks presents itself. What if something unexpected happens between signing and close? That new sort of risk, in turn, will have to be negotiated into the definitive agreements, thus unfortunately adding complexity, time and expense.

Hence, it behooves the seller to get a firm commitment for a simultaneous sign and close early on in the acquisition process. The buyer may have assumed that the deal's completion will be sequential rather than simultaneous—maybe because that's what they're accustomed to. So it's good to make the simultaneous understanding explicit. In my experience, both sellers and buyers will go for a simultaneous sign and close, even if they haven't always given much thought beforehand to this aspect of the deal's consummation.

If it comes to pass that a sequential sign and close is required, push to have the shortest time-to-close, and the fewest number of closing conditions.

Announcing the acquisition

The announcement of a transaction plays a role in how both sides approach the endgame. As a general rule, I prefer to hold any announcement until the deal is completely closed. For regulatory reasons, however, a publicly traded buyer will have to announce a material transaction upon signing a definitive agreement (and sometimes even earlier in the process). The risk—mostly for the seller, unfortunately—is that the announcement may bring forth scrutiny, claimants or other interference that could cause the transaction to fall apart.

At times, an early announcement of the acquisition or something on the path to the acquisition (like a major partnership) can serve to bind the buyer to the seller. If the buyer commits publicly to both a direction and the startup's role in this new strategy, that commitment creates a visible bond that the buyer may not want to see broken, nor have to explain the dissolution of, later.

Lastly, it may come to pass that the transaction is never announced at all! Every day, many small startup acquisitions are quietly completed with barely a murmur made in the market. Buyers may prefer this to reduce visibility into their strategy and lower the risk of a third party taking issue and making a posttransaction claim.

D&O tail coverage

A final note on closing: Ask your attorneys if you should consider purchasing an extension to your directors and officers ("D&O") insurance (posttransaction extensions are typically called "tail coverage"). Once the deal is closed, many D&O policies end and it may make sense for you to extend your coverage for some additional period of time.

Faith in the deal

We've come a long way in this book. One of the reviewers of an earlier draft commented: "Reading all this, I have no idea how any of these deals ever get done."

As I tell people, "Acquisitions are like babies. Each one is a miracle. Fortunately, they happen all the time!"

Sometimes they have twists and turns. Sometimes it looks like all hope is lost. If it's a strong thesis, however, and you've approached things the right way, there's a good chance it'll come together.

These deals require a bit of faith. Faith that your buyer will ultimately see reason, your stakeholders will align their interests, and the combination does in fact make sense. If you have faith in the deal, you'll find it takes a bit of the pressure off each of the decisions and variables will fall into place. When times get tough, take a deep breath and stay calm. If the deal is meant to happen, it probably will. If it doesn't, life will go on.

Chapter 11

Flotsam and jetsam

We're not done yet, there's still just a wee bit more to discuss

There are a few more topics that didn't quite fit anywhere else in the book but are worth taking a quick spin through.

Should we hire professional advisors or investment bankers?

Absolutely, sometimes.

I wrote this book from the perspective of you doing this all on your own. I thought that would be easier to understand than discussing the potential interplay between you and your advisors.

In my experience, the decision to hire advisors will typically come down to three factors: your specific situation, you, and your would-be advisor.

Having a clear-headed view of your situation is the first and topmost priority. If you follow the approach offered in this book and a deal emerges, and your buyer has a clear thesis for your magic box, then you may be quite able to hammer out simple and friendly terms on your own without the use of professional advisors. You, a good attorney, an experienced board member and a copy of the MBP may be all that's needed.

If, on the other hand, you want to put yourself into MBP mode without having to master all the ins-and-outs on your own, then advisors can be a big help. Or if an opportunity presents itself that looks complicated, with significant areas of negotiation, then a third-party advisor may become quite relevant to your efforts. Even more so, if the process is going to involve multiple potential buyers simultaneously.

In addition, because these deals are so intensely personal, and so much is based on trust between the buyer and seller, it's important for you not to play "bad cop." Let the advisor assume that role and handle the tough topics. You will need to make a self-evaluation of your skills. If you've read this book, and the nuances and complexities of pulling all of this together give you the heebie-jeebies, then engaging an advisor will make a lot of sense.

Which brings us to the advisor. There are some great advisors and there are some not so great ones. Here are the areas I'd recommend you consider as you evaluate professional advisors and investment bankers:

- Articulation
- Relationships over networks
- Startup experience

Articulation

Much of the value of your startup lies in the future and in the effective articulation of your magic box. You want an advisor who can not only help you fine-tune your story but also articulate it well on his own. This is important because you likely won't be able to make every call yourself nor attend every meeting. You want your advisory team to help carry a significant part of the outreach load.

Relationships over networks

If you go to enough parties, you can build a pretty big network pretty quickly, but real relationships take years to form. They are built upon trust and shared experience. No one knows everyone, but you're looking for the advisory team consisting of people with history and relationships with key people at relevant PSPs.

Startup experience

By now, I hope you've come to realize that startup acquisitions have their own idiosyncrasies and dynamics. Some advisors understand how to work with magic boxes; others, only Popsicles. You should look for an advisory team that has successfully completed more than a few startup acquisitions.

The relationship with your advisor

If you decide that an investment bank or professional advisor makes sense, my advice is to keep the relationship simple. There's a temptation to attempt to overengineer the economic model of the engagement. More often than not, these efforts to optimize end up misaligning interests. Set up a simple and clear relationship with your advisor and keep the economics very clean.

Two ways startups misguidedly attempt to modify their engagements with their advisors are carve-outs and tiered fee structures.

Carve-outs

Startups will often feel the advisor should receive a lower fee for transactions completed with buyers with whom they already have a relationship. My short answer to carve-outs is that if you feel your advisor won't add a few percentage points in value to any transaction, you're considering the wrong advisor.

But the deeper issue with carve-outs is that they misalign the startup's and the advisor's interests. For example, let's say there are two potential buyers interested in buying a startup. Buyer A is willing to pay $100 million; buyer B is willing to pay $75 million. The advisor's engagement agreement with the startup says that for any transaction, except with buyer A (because the startup has been working with buyer A for years), the fee will be calculated at 5 percent of the transaction value. The fee on a transaction with buyer A will be calculated at the reduced rate of 2.5 percent.

In this structure, the advisor's fee on a transaction with buyer A is $2.5 million; with buyer B, it is $3.75 million. The advisor makes a 50 percent greater fee if the company ends up with the buyer willing to pay $25 million less. That's a misalignment if I ever saw one!

Tiered fee structures

Along with carve-outs, many startups want to create an incentive structure that they believe will drive the advisor to achieve the highest possible price. To this end, the startups will seek to pay the advisor based on a formula whereby the advisor's fee increases at various hurdle points. There are three problems with tiered fee structures.

First, as a practical matter most buyers are going to want to see your engagement agreement with your advisor (it's very hard to keep them shielded from the buyer in deep due diligence). At exactly the wrong moment, you have to give the buyer a great deal of insight into your valuation expectations.

This "visibility" issue also applies to the carve-outs mentioned in the last section. You don't really want to tip your hat as to other potential buyers (and bring up questions as to why they didn't buy you!).

Second, tiered fee structures create the incentive for your advisor to push for higher-risk, higher-reward acquisition scenarios. If the advisor can make a much larger fee on a high-risk potential buyer (but one with a low likelihood of actually closing), he may pay too little attention to higher-probability but lower-priced options.

Also, as we've discussed throughout this book, price is only one of many moving parts in an acquisition. Going "all-in" on price can have significant negative consequences on other aspects of the acquisition. Ultimately, tiered fee structures don't comport with a holistic approach to the transaction and can leave a trail of failed deals.

Third, in transactions that are anything but cash-at-close (which is a great many transactions when you factor in those that consist of equity, debt, retention, earnouts, etc.), determining the "price" of the deal for advisor fee calculation purposes can be challenging. This problem is then exacerbated if there is the added dimension of substantially different, price-driven, fee structures. At exactly the moment you want to be on the same page as your advisor, you're instead fighting with each other over a convoluted fee calculation.

As has been noted many times in this book, the startup acquisition process is complicated enough without adding self-inflicted injuries. Do everything you can to drive toward simplicity, even in your relationship with your advisor.

Being a good acquisition

The deal is done. But you may not be. In most cases, the team is going to continue on with the acquiring company. Creating a new innovation is a journey. The acquisition is just one step in that journey. The innovation is now going to move to a bigger stage and have the chance to change the world. You may have just made a lot of money, but that doesn't mean your work is done. Your work may in fact be just beginning.

Many entrepreneurs have a hard time transitioning from startup mode to big company mode. But make the effort. Work to see your innovation reach its full potential. Your name will forever be associated with it, so have it perceived in the halls of history to have been a great idea, great startup and great acquisition. This may mean you stay engaged for months. It may even mean years or decades. You'll know when you've done all you can. But take a long view. Do what you can to ensure your buyer gets full value for what they paid. You'll feel better about yourself and be better viewed by the world.

There's a positive wrinkle in all of this. In successful acquisitions, the team members can, over the course of their time with the buyer, create more wealth in their roles in the acquirer's organization than they did from the proceeds of the deal that brought them there. Becoming a member of the leadership team at your buyer may just be the logical next step in your career.

Surviving a blown deal

It happens. A deal gets to the one-yard line and falls apart. It happens for big reasons. It happens for small reasons. Sometimes you can see it coming. Sometimes the hammer strikes out of the blue.

It's never easy and sometimes can be excruciating. If you generally followed the methodology in this book, you should have a "deal didn't happen, but it's OK, onward" narrative into which your stakeholders and team have previously contributed, and can now fit. But that doesn't mean it's easy for you. In fact, it's hardest for you.

However, the world keeps turning. And that sentiment isn't just feel-good mumbo jumbo. I've seen acquisitions fall apart and then something even better emerges later on. Everyone may then be exceedingly happy that you astutely didn't close the initial deal!

Sometimes your job is to just keep the ball bouncing, however you can. Hang in there. It may feel crappy right now, but nothing is more fun than an epic comeback.

Hello buyers, we see you!

You did it, didn't you? You bought this book. You peeked behind the curtain. The cat is out of the bag now!

Well, here are a few thoughts for you as well.

A balanced approach

If a startup you think you may want to acquire is willing to patiently walk the road with you, maybe you should show a little patience too.

More often than not, it's not the end of the world if a buyer doesn't end up acquiring a startup that at first seemed attractive. And if losing the deal would end the world, then for goodness' sake don't play games. Put together an offer they can't refuse. It'll be worth it.

For the buyer, this-or-that startup acquisition is typically filling some sort of gap or advancing you down some path. It will be based on a big idea, but in a macro, corporate sense, the acquisition is often tactical for you. However, the acquisition is a horse of a different color for the startup. On that side of the fence, it's anything but tactical. Hence, if the startup seems to be following something close to the MBP, and working with you in a measured and even-keeled way, consider matching the pace.

In my experience, most buyers underappreciate the importance to the seller of a stable and reliable counterparty. Startups typically don't want deals to fall apart, and the risk of changing buyer horses in the middle of the deal river is huge to the seller. Once the transaction closing process has begun in earnest, most startups would like to get the deal done with the buyer currently engaged. As the buyer, if you keep the deal moving briskly, you will find that in all likelihood it closes pretty quickly.

Exploring isn't the same as closing

While you are in the exploratory phase (and not yet in the closing process), keep the tempo of the deal on your side in sync with your real level of interest and commitment. Over the long run, by not rushing to lock up the seller, you may lose a deal or two. But the deals you do complete will be with people who genuinely want to join forces with you, not the ones you quickly lock into an arranged marriage, or worse, a hurried engagement with no union!

Don't sit on the lamp and kill the genie

When it comes to startup acquisitions, there's such a thing as cutting too good a deal. Heavy-handed negotiating tactics can have cascading negative consequences. Particularly for you, the buyer. You are buying a magic box. You want to enhance, and not extinguish, the magic.

It may seem to certain of your constituents that everything possible should be done to derisk the deal. Yet, adding complexity (think earnouts) can create challenges for both sides. If this is a startup you really want to acquire, create a simple deal, move fast and get it done. A complex deal structure, in and of itself, increases the likelihood of the deal falling apart before close. Worse, the resulting postacquisition operating environment could work counter to what you were trying to achieve through the acquisition in the first place. Excessive derisking can in fact become a formula for failure.

Separate market participation risk from acquisition risk

As we discussed at length in the section on risk allocation, expanding your position in a market brings risks. Don't attempt to transfer those risks to the startup you're acquiring.

The startup's role is to save you development time, not underwrite your participation in the market.

You are, of course, entitled to full, comprehensive disclosure and reasonable measures to cover unforeseen obligations. But in terms of participation in a new market, that's your buy-versus-build call, and you need to make your own assessments and calculations as to what may happen down the line.

If you're really worried, buy insurance, from, like, an actual insurance company!

Complete the mojo circle by realizing that the buy side could benefit from a little Zen as well.

Conclusion

You did it, you're MBP certified!

I hope your view of startup acquisitions is radically different now from what it was a couple hundred pages ago. And, that you appreciate that startup acquisitions aren't over for you or your acquirer, when the deal closes. In many ways, they're just beginning.

While the fact that you and your buyer are going to have to join together to get your magic box to the top of the mountain has wide-ranging implications on the entire process, it's also the indicator of the amount of faith being put in your startup and you.

I hope now you appreciate that many of the things conventional wisdom and even your intuition might have told you to do are exactly opposite to the things that you should do. Term sheets are mirages; you are most often the casualty of a bidding war; and earnouts have a way of turning into fool's gold, to name a few.

Remember, the MBP is a holistic approach, from how you enter the room, the creation of your narrative, use of your data room, setting of price, definition of terms and finally closing. It doesn't work in pieces; it only works as a whole.

But it does work, I use it every day.

Backstory

My hope is that this book will be useful for startup board members, investors, advisors, attorneys and other stakeholders. But, it isn't written for them. It's for you, the entrepreneur. You are the one in the arena, with all eyes upon you. The one who has to actually make the moves required to win the game.

Recently, I got off what must have been the tenth call that week from a startup founder trying to figure out how best to approach a potential acquisition scenario. Bambi (my wife, collaborator, muse) asked if I really had the time to take all these calls.

She wasn't suggesting that I shouldn't help these callers, but just that I needed to come up with a more efficient approach. I get introduced to what seems like an endless stream of entrepreneurs, and, from what I can tell, folks with whom they can discuss the strategies and dynamics of startup acquisition are hard to find.

The Magic Box Paradigm represents the distillation of my approach to startup acquisitions; it's what I reference on all those calls.

The Magic Box Paradigm is for startups, sort of...

I've never really cared for the "startup" moniker. For one thing, the term connotes newness, and an innovative organization isn't necessarily new. I've known companies that have taken a decade to get off the ground and many great new ideas that have emerged from century-old organizations.

For purposes of the MBP, I'd like to widen the definition of startup a little to include not only independent new companies but also innovative divisions of existing companies and even teams working on new products deep inside of established corporations. "Startup" means a collection of people creating new, innovative offerings.

To the extent we're discussing startups as companies, this book only contemplates them as private companies (public companies have additional complexities into which we don't have time to dive here).

Context

Business books are too often too long. This one is pretty short. It's hopefully an easy read too. But there's a price to pay. Readers must read these pages in sequence and understand references to earlier concepts. A lot of detail has been sacrificed in favor of brevity. Generally applicable ideas take center stage, with most corner cases having been rounded out of the book.

Don't think of it as a fully comprehensive guide. It's a primer on some of the big topics and a guidebook for successfully preparing for and navigating through common acquisition situations. It's also not a textbook, and it doesn't offer legal advice. Instead, it's a hybrid of philosophy and process.

My narrative draws on not only my professional experience advising startups, but also on what I've observed with friends' startups and have learned from colleagues, advice-seekers and war-story-swappers. I've been fortunate to have had a bountiful supply of patterns to match.

This book is more about form than substance. As it says in Ecclesiastes, "There's nothing new under the sun." I'm sure most, if not all, readers will have at some point developed a presentation or negotiated a deal.

Included are unexpected techniques for what you thought you already knew how to do. Everyone can swing a golf club, but how that swing is made differentiates a duffer from a Master's champion.

Just a couple more thoughts on context. Most of my career has been spent working with digital businesses. If your startup isn't a digital business, then this book is probably going to be light on topics that are important to your situation. The book is also written from a largely U.S. vantage point. It may of course be necessary to adapt some of its recommendations to the particular circumstances of your region or industry.

The tools and frameworks will point you in the right direction. This is all intended to be a starting point for conversations with your board, stakeholders and advisors. I want it to give you a solid foundation from which you can develop your own perspective and devise an approach that will best suit your situation and you.

Lastly, I attempted to limit my use of inside-baseball, startup jargon. However, in places I do use terms that are common in the startup community. I hope I was able to find a balance between accessible language for those new to startups and efficient communication for startup veterans.

This book is approached as though it's a fluid conversation between us.

Talk back at www.advsr.com/mbp

I look forward to hearing from you!

About the Author

At the start of my career I was fortunate to have had the opportunity to cofound two technology companies. One ended up being quite successful and was acquired. The other had a good run but was unable to survive the burst of the first internet bubble. As an entrepreneur I've been part of teams that have created innovative products and services. I've seen how swiftly success can come, and go.

Since the early 2000s I've largely worked as an advisor to startups. Today my professional activities leverage three platforms: Advsr, a growing network of entrepreneurs; Ackrell Capital, a boutique investment bank; and Vator, an online community for startups and investors.

I earned an MBA from a joint program of UC Berkeley's Haas School of Business and Columbia's Graduate School of Business. Prior to that, I earned a BA in Philosophy from UC Davis with minors in both History and English.

Made in the USA
San Bernardino, CA
21 October 2016